S.Sidwell

E.ftgate

Corbelch

Bedford haufe

Steuen

S.Mary

St.eters

S.Perols

Bishop's palleg

Frenche

S.Georg

South gate

the Mault line

Cork Beare

Radfort place

Holloway

S.Leonard

S.Mary Stepps

Water gate

Crane Seller

S.Leonard w

West gate

The Kay

New hauen

CIVITAS EXONIÆ
(vulgo Excester) VRBS
PRIMARIA IN CO:
MITATV DEVONIÆ

Floyers hayes

S.Thomas

EXETER
PAST

'Near the Quay' by John White Abbott (1803)

EXETER PAST

Hazel Mary Harvey

Phillimore

1996

Published by
PHILLIMORE & CO. LTD.,
Shopwyke Manor Barn, Chichester, West Sussex

ISBN 1 86077 006 1

Printed and bound in Great Britain by
BIDDLES LTD.
Guildford, Surrey

Yet poets too by Isca dream;
Rich meadows kiss her sparkling face,
And ancient walls o'erhang her stream,
And peopled towns her borders grace.

from *The River Exe*
by John Herman Merivale (1779-1884)

Contents

List of Illustrations

Frontispiece: 'Near the Quay' by John White Abbott (1803)

Acknowledgments

The following institutions supplied illustrations and/or permission to use them: Bodleian Library, Oxford, 45; Devon and Exeter Institution, 19, 21-25, 27, 35, 39, 40, 43, 46, 48, 52, 54, 59, 61, 63, 64, 67-70, 81, 83, 85, 90, 91, 93, 97, 125, 126; Exeter Archaeology, 3, 4, 6, 7, 13, 20; Exeter Cathedral Library, 10, 14, 50, 87-89; Exeter Civic Society, 8, 60, 64, 135, 137, 138; Exeter University, 141; *Express and Echo*, 56, 103, 111, 114, 122, 127-29, 131-33, 139, 140, 142; Isca Collection, 56; National Railway Museum, York, 94, 95; Ny Carlsberg Glyptotek, Copenhagen, 1; Railway Studies Collection, Newton Abbot Library (Devon County Council), 82; Royal Albert Memorial Museum (Exeter City Council), frontispiece, 11, 31, 71, 124; Victoria and Albert Museum, 44; Walter Scott (Bradford) Ltd., 130; Westcountry Studies Library (Devon County Council), 26, 55, 84, 86 and endpaper maps.

Illustrations have also been taken from Dr. T. Shapter, *The History of the Cholera in Exeter in 1832* (1849).

The author is indebted to P.V. Pitman for allowing reproduction of her drawings (78, 80) and for lending postcards; Monica Hoare for lending postcards published by her grandfather's firm, Worth & Co.; Elaine M. Goodwin, 12; Mrs. G. Price, 127; the Sclater family, 107, 108; Nigel Watts 79; Bob and Betty Youngson, 119. She also wishes to record her appreciation of the generous help given by the editor of the *Express & Echo*, Rachael Campey, and the paper's nostalgia specialist, Geoff Worrall; and the friendly cooperation of John Allan, Jane Baker, Roy and Monty Chisholm, Aileen Fox, Catherine and Ivor Jewell, Ian Maxted, Richard Parker, Michael G. Smith, Sheila Stirling, Robert Sweetland, Peter W. Thomas, Ray Vail, Gilbert Venn, Peter Weddell, Peter Wiseman and Michael Woollacott. Her husband David word-processed the text without grumbling too much or introducing many deliberate misprints.

Chapter 1

Britons and Romans

Exeter lies where the invading Romans built a fortress in about A.D. 50, on a steep-sided spur overlooking the river-crossing, where a natural shelf served as a quay. In A.D. 43 the emperor Claudius had sent forces to subdue the south of Britain. His general Vespasian and the Second Augustan legion had worked their way from east to west, capturing a total of 19 strongholds before they arrived here. Medieval chronicles report a seven-day siege at 'the camp on the hill by the great wood' before the local British king and the Roman commander came to terms.

The inhabitants of the western peninsula were called Dumnonii. They lived in small farming settlements among the wooded hills, raising cattle, sheep, goats and grain. Their major defensive forts were several miles north and east of the future site of Exeter, but they had a camp a mile north of the river-crossing, and a small trading-post near the river bank. The prehistoric ridgeway, the Icknield Way, which ran across the whole breadth of Britain, came along the spine which is now occupied by Sidwell Street and High Street, to terminate on the cliff-top above the river.

Strabo the geographer, writing about half a century earlier, recorded that the British exported gold, silver, iron, grain, hides, slaves and hunting dogs; it rained a lot, and on fine days it was foggy; the British were long-limbed, towering over the tallest Romans; they kept their cattle in clearings in the woods. 'The forests are their cities', he wrote.

The name of the Dumnonii may come from the Celtic word for 'deep', 'mysterious', and may denote worshippers of the Mysterious God or dwellers in the deep valleys, or (like the names of many tribes) it may simply mean

1 Here the mature Vespasian is portrayed, after he had become emperor in A.D. 69. At the time of the Roman Conquest of Britain he had been recently promoted to command of a legion. His previous responsibility had been to keep the streets of Rome free of litter and filth.

1

'us here', 'the people', as opposed to 'them'. 'They' at this point were the Roman invaders, who seem to have met with little resistance after the initial siege. The Dumnonii were proud and fierce, with their own kings, but they were not tightly organised. They did not issue their own coinage, although neighbouring tribes did.

Vespasian's camp-prefect, Publius Anicius Maximus, supervised the construction of a temporary fortlet above the quay. He or his successor, Poenius Postumus, oversaw the

2 The bend where upper Paul Street meets Gandy Street preserves the line of the path where the guard patrolled just inside the fortress ramparts. The fortress boundary has also been excavated in Friernhay Street and elsewhere, and subsidence cracks in the museum and in St Stephen's church reveal that they stand on the fortress ditch.

building of a full-scale military fortress, enclosing 38 acres, on the top of the spur. The Roman military presence lasted for 20-30 years, with all the shouting and clatter of barracks, workshops, hospital, kitchens, and stabling for the horses and mules. There was a hill-top signal station to the north (near the British camp) where beacons could be seen instantly from as far as Dorchester. Its ditch is still visible from the air, outlined by the trees round the practice yard of the present riding-school. Among the timber buildings of the main fortress, a lofty stone bath-house was constructed in A.D. 55, with mosaic floors, and walls panelled in Purbeck marble, apsed at each end. Channels brought water from springs on the ridge to the east.

During Boudicca's rebellion in A.D. 60-1 Poenius Postumus failed to respond to a call for reinforcements, and then killed himself for shame, because he had denied his legion this chance of gaining glory. In *c.*75-80 the legion dismantled the fortress palisades and carried them to Wales. The military bath-house was demolished. In its place there rose grand stone civic buildings for the regional *civitas* capital, Isca Dumnoniorum. A combined forum and basilica complex accommodated municipal offices and shops, with public baths nearby.

Isca was the Celtic name for the river rich in salmon. The fortress had been completely Roman, neat and tidy, under military discipline, with officers from Italy and soldiers from various parts of the empire housed in close-packed rectangular barrack blocks. The British who settled outside its walls had built wattle-and-daub workshops and huts in which food remains and broken pottery lay messily mingled with industrial waste from working bronze and enamel, and leather scraps and lumps of iron slag. In contrast, the town which succeeded the fortress must be described as Romano-British, since it assimilated enterprising individuals enticed in from life in the countryside, who set up stalls and workshops along the streets; some of them eventually participated in local government as council members, magistrates and tax-gatherers, settling disputes, collecting market-tolls and making sure that the streets were clean.

Until *c.*160 the town of Isca had no outer defences. Cemeteries lay beside the main exit roads (two on the sites of the future churches

3 Excavations in 1972 on the site of St Mary Major revealed the legionary bath-house from *c*.A.D. 55, with under-floor heating, cut through 50 years later by the walls of the administrative *basilica* of the Romano-British town. The substantial remains were recorded and grassed over. The Royal Albert Museum has a comprehensive display of the finds.

4 This mosaic floor from a central building has a guilloche pattern in red, white and grey-blue. The cubes were cut from old tiles, East Devon limestone and local siderite. Similar materials were used for the mosaic floor of the earlier bath-house, where one fragment shows hooves, perhaps from a depiction of the insignia of the Second Augusta legion, Pegasus.

of St Sidwell and St David, and one outside the south gate). Vineyards and orchards covered the sunny slopes. The defences of the military fortress had been levelled. The ditch had been forgotten when a grand town-house was built on the future site of St Catherine's almshouses. Part of the mosaic floor of its corridor was found in modern times: it had folded at right angles into the fortress ditch. Traces of another town-house found near Carfax in 1994, in the middle of the High Street, show that the Roman street grid did not coincide with the modern one.

Some time after 160 an earth rampart was thrown up to enclose 93 acres, including the red volcanic knob at the north-east corner. (The earth bank survives behind the wall in Rougemont Gardens, in the garden of the Bishop's Palace, and in the grounds of 14 The Close.) After *c.*200 the rampart was reinforced with massive stone walls, over 15 ft. high and 9 ft. thick. Timber gatehouses were replaced by stone ones, which have also long since gone, although the outlines of the Roman south gate have recently been marked out in brickwork in the pavement of South Street. The walls themselves, generally embedded in the work of later generations, can still be seen in an almost complete circuit. They run along the crest of the low cliff above the river, make a right-angled turn to run east above the deep valley of the northern brook, and circle the volcanic knob to reach Eastgate. On the south-eastern side the terrain is less precipitous, sloping more gently to the southern brook. Roman masonry is visible in many stretches, mainly in the lower courses. Herringbone work is exposed just to the left of the archway which leads from Rougemont Gardens to Northernhay. The massive thickness of the core can be seen near Maddocks Row in Paul Street car-park, and characteristic squared blocks in Northernhay Gardens, in Post Office Street, Quay Lane and many other places.

5 Squared blocks of purple volcanic stone quarried from Rougemont can be seen in several stretches of the surviving walls (here in Northernhay Gardens). The stone has a characteristic honeycomb surface.

The line of the Roman walls still defines Exeter's centre, forming an irregular rhomboid, or, as John Hooker put it in the 16th century, 'It is not altogether fowre square but decline the somewhat towards a rowndeness'. In the 18 centuries since the wall was built the city has engulfed neighbouring villages and even two towns (St Thomas and Topsham), but the original site of Roman Isca provides the civic focus, containing castle, cathedral, Guildhall, Civic Centre, law courts, main shopping areas, libraries, museums and historic churches.

To judge by the number of coins found, the Romano-British town flourished as a centre of trade. From A.D. 212 no distinction was drawn between Roman and British—if they were free men they were full citizens of the empire. The town's population grew from about one thousand to twice or three times as many by the late fourth century. There were plentiful supplies of grain, vegetables, dairy foods and fish. Venison was enjoyed more widely than it would be in the middle ages, and large amounts of beef, pork, duck and oysters too. Native hazelnuts and introduced walnuts, with plums, apples, grapes, mulberries and cherries, were all available.

There is evidence that Christianity has been practised in Exeter for over 1,600 years. The religion had gained tolerance under the Emperor Constantine in 313. A *chi-rho* sign scratched on a sherd from a fourth-century black-burnished cooking pot has been found in South Street. The little church of St Pancras has been rebuilt several times, but its dedication is to a fourth-century Roman martyr, and its alignment seems to predate the medieval street-grid.

In about A.D. 380 the forum was remodelled, but by then the town was beginning to decline. Fewer coins came in to be mislaid or deliberately buried. When the Roman administration withdrew from Britain in 410, Isca's buildings began to fall into disrepair. Rubbish pits were dug in the centre of town. The paved streets disappeared under briars and brambles. Furze and fern reclaimed the slopes. Some British families continued to occupy the north-west corner inside the walls, where the ground drops steeply on two sides. They had lived in this area before the Romans arrived, and they stayed on after the Romans left. This quarter continued to be called Britayne for centuries afterwards.

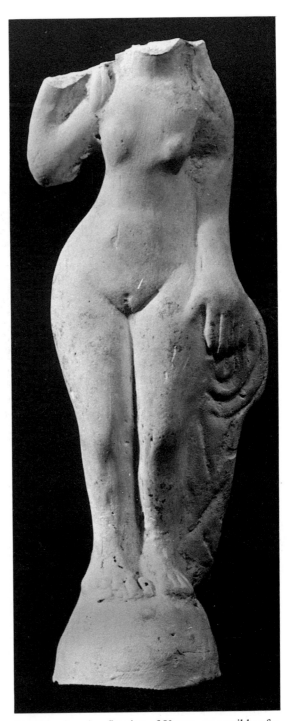

6 This pipe-clay figurine of Venus, or possibly of a Celtic fertility goddess, was found in a late second-century context in the Trichay Street area (but almost immediately stolen). Many similar figures were made in France in the preceding century and were widely distributed.

7 This miniature portrait head, found in the Goldsmith Street area in a fourth-century context, was probably made in the first century A.D. from white Mediterranean marble. It is as small as a pear but precisely carved to show a bald dome, lined forehead and deep-set eyes. It may have been set up as a memorial bust in a private home.

It was the British Dumnonians who maintained Christian practice in Exeter between the decline of the Roman town and the arrival of the Saxons. A few fifth- to seventh-century graves have been found in the area of the demolished forum, alongside a building which may have been used as a church. Of the many medieval city churches, those dedicated to Celtic missionary saints (Kerrian, Petrock, Pol de Leon) stood near the British quarter. But the British had never been true city-dwellers. Isca came and went, 'a mere parcel' cut out of the royal estates. The kings of Dumnonia probably continued to hold their assemblies at the traditional landmark tree at Wonford, a mile east of Exeter, where the north-south ridgeway crosses the east-west route. A church was later built beside the yew tree on the knoll, but the tree continued to be respected for its significance and antiquity until 1541. In that year the church tower was rebuilt and the tree was felled, but a side-shoot sprang up, which is itself now a sizeable tree on age-old roots. It may be regarded as the Head Tree which gave Wonford its nickname of Heavitree.

The Romans left imposing reminders of their centuries here: squared masonry, mosaic floors, coins, pottery, sculpture, the city walls and the remains of the bath-house. Because of this, and because we know about them from their literature and inscriptions, their history has overshadowed that of the British population, whose 'greener' life-style left few tangible traces. The Dumnonii have not provided any of the illustrations for this chapter. But it should be remembered that the British were here long before the Romans, they played a full part in the Romano-British town, and they were still here for centuries afterwards, even after the Saxon settlers arrived.

Chapter 2

Saxons and Danes

From the middle of the sixth century the West Saxons were trying to expand into Dumnonian territory. Many British emigrated to Brittany during this period, possibly after poor harvests, or illness, or because they had been driven from their farms and their men had been killed. The chronicles record battles but do not give details of Saxon settlement. For centuries the British had occupied the high ground, for safety, and also because the lighter upland soil was easier to till. The ploughs of the Saxon incomers could cope with the heavy 'red-brick' clay of the east Devon valleys. The landscape pattern still visible today—Saxon villages in the valleys, surrounded by large fields, alongside older British farmsteads on the slopes—reveals the state of play when the fighting stopped. Exeter stands at the border between the two types of soil and the two ways of life. At this time, the town was home to only a few British families. Sometimes more gathered there to hold the walls against the Saxons: in 568 against Cealwin, king of Wessex, and in 632 against Penda, king of Mercia. In 658 the British lost: Cenwealh of Wessex beat them at Pinhoe and then took Exeter. Three years later he beat them again, near Crediton. It may have been Cenwealh, baptised in 644, in possession of the Devon royal estates since 658, who, with the fervour of the newly converted, built the first church at Wonford next to the head tree. In 670 he founded an abbey at *Exanceastre*, possibly requisitioning the small British church in the central burial yard.

Some ten years later the small Saxon boy who was to become famous as Boniface, apostle to the Germans, came from Crediton to receive his early education under Abbot Wolfhard here. The long life of Boniface is fully documented: his further education, his journeys to Rome, the chain of monasteries which he founded in the German forests, his personal correspondence, and his martyrdom at a great age at the hands of the Frisians. (His cousin Walpurgis who also took Germany as her mission field is said to have come from Devon too.)

The solidity of the record of the life of Boniface makes his alleged contemporary, Sidwell, seem a creature of fairy-tales: a devout Saxon maiden who was beheaded by her father's farm-workers in the fields outside

8 The figure of St Sidwell on the store next to the church is by Frederick Irving, 1969.

Eastgate, 'since when God has performed miracles there at her shrine'. In 930 King Athelstan confirmed ownership of her remains to the minster. In 1072 Leofric included them in his list of cathedral relics. By 1335 Bishop Grandisson had expanded Sidwell's story into a full-scale *legenda*, with a jealous stepmother, a miraculous healing spring breaking from the ground where the girl's head had fallen, and light shining from the corpse. Grandisson was writing 650 years after the alleged events, by which time the Middle English syllables of Sidwell's name formed a convenient rebus on the murder weapon (scythe) and miraculous result (well). These symbols feature in her stained-glass portrait in the 14th-century east window of the cathedral. But the pun would not have worked in Anglo-Saxon. The name was recorded as *Sedefulle* in 1013 in a tourist guide to the resting-places of the saints. *Sedefulle* is a descriptive epithet, 'full of virtue'. Rational thought suggests that Sidwell never existed as an individual. The ridge outside Eastgate has always been bursting with springs for geological reasons. These springs were certainly used by the Romans, and doubtless by the British before them. Severed heads and holy wells played leading rôles in pre-Christian Celtic religion. The Sidwell legend most likely arose from the systematic christianisation of pagan holy sites and pagan festivals which the church undertook from the seventh century onwards. Boniface chopped down Thor's sacred oak in the German forest. In the same spirit, Exeter's bishops imposed a Christian identity on the pre-Christian holy well outside the Eastgate.

The Venerable Bede described the forests of the south-west in the eighth century as full of deer, boar and man-eating wolves. The Saxon kings often visited Exanceastre to enjoy hunting in the steep wooded valleys north of the town which formed its 'door-yard', or possession outside the gates. Duryard is named in Domesday as city property, and it kept its unusual status until the early 1700s, when the land was sold for development. For centuries it was a valuable source of timber, particularly oak. It is now a protected valley park, from which deer still leap into the neighbouring gardens.

King Ine of Wessex asserted dominance over King Geraint of Dumnonia soon after 700, and the bishop of Sherborne negotiated with Geraint about standardising the timing of Easter celebrations. But each Saxon king had to make a fresh agreement with the British. A century later they held out against King Egbert, from 800 until 816, before agreeing to the usual arrangement: that they could continue to live under their own laws if they paid an annual tribute.

In the early ninth century, Vikings began to raid the south coast. In 851 the men of *Defenascire* drove them off. In 876 the 'Danish pagans' came riding overland from Dorset, pursued by King Alfred and his men. The Danes reached Exeter, and overwintered inside the walls. The following year, Alfred drove them out, and took steps to keep them out of the country. He ordered longships to be built: the shipwrights of the Exe thus helped inaugurate England's royal navy. He established a stronghold or *burh* in each of four royal possessions in Devonshire—Exeter, Totnes, Lydford and Barnstaple—where the burgesses paid dues direct to the crown. Exeter's Roman walls were repaired. Parts of the modern street plan may date from this time. Present-day Fore Street may preserve the width and straightness of Alfred's new main street. Gandy Street, St Martin's Lane and Catherine Street are surviving examples of the narrower side-streets which formed a regular grid. The blocks were divided into rectangular 'burgage plots' of equal size, each with a frontage onto the street. Alfred established a mint for silver pennies in each *burh*. He made an impromptu gift of the church at Exeter, with its possessions 'in Saxon and Cornish areas', to his friend and biographer, the bishop from Wales, Asser. The western diocese was still based in Sherborne, but when Asser died in 909 a bishop's seat was established in Crediton.

Alfred's daughter was given in marriage to an ealdorman of Mercia. Ties with Mercia may explain the dedication to the Mercian martyr St Osyth of a cross outside Westgate.

In 893 the Danes could not penetrate the new defences and besieged Exeter instead, until they heard that Alfred was coming to disperse them, and they fled.

Alfred's son, Edward the Elder, chose Exeter for his law-making conference of earls and priests (*Witanagemot*) in 918. Alfred's grandson, Athelstan, held royal councils in

9 *Right.* 'Toisa's Cross' is a late-Saxon granite praying-cross the height of a man, tapering slightly, and carved on all four sides with interlaced patterns. 'T Oisa' is thought to be a local pronunciation of St Osyth. This may be the cross described as broken in 1316, when it stood outside Westgate near the river-crossing.

10 *Far right.* Incantations and etiquette meet in the Anglo-Saxon maxims written on vellum in square minuscules on this page of the 10th-century *Exeter Book.*

> FROST shall freeze, fire burn wood, earth grow ... and mighty God shall break frost's fetters.

At the foot of the page:

> In handing round the mead-cup she must quickly reach the first drink to her lord.

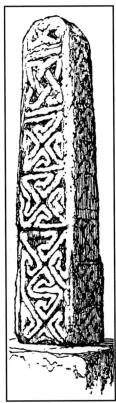

Exeter in 928 and 935. Until then, the British were still occupying their quarter, under their own laws, which ranked equally with English law. Athelstan now tidied up the town by expelling 'that filthy race' to beyond the Tamar (including their king, Howell); he repaired the walls and added defensive towers. Present-day Athelstan Road runs along part of his eastern defensive dyke.

Athelstan also refounded the minster, giving it 26 manors and a third of his large collection of relics, including fragments of the Holy Cross, of the Lord's tomb, His garment, the manger, Longinus' spear, the table of the last supper, St Andrew's staff, a stone which St Silvin had carried to Rome three times, and a piece of the burning bush.

The minster's scriptorium produced fine manuscripts, and it is now thought that the 'large English book with everything written in verse' known as the *Exeter Book* was written there. This is one of only four surviving collections of Old English poetry. It has preserved dozens of jokey Anglo-Saxon riddles about such things as the cuckoo, rising dough,

a ship and a weather-cock. There are also melancholy elegies. One, *The Ruin*, seems to describe the remains of the Roman baths from half a millennium before and their crumbling walls—lichen-grey and stained with red, broken arches and streams of heated water. 'Bright were the buildings, many the bath-chambers, high were the gables, great the sound of merriment ... '.

In 968 King Edgar the Peaceful sent a group of monks led by Abbot Sidemann to reform the minster. Henceforth the scribes were to copy only theological texts. Sidemann was tutor to Edgar's son Edward, so the martyr-king may have been a schoolboy here. Perhaps they let him read the riddles. Edgar also reformed the mint, in 973. From that time, all coins had the king's head on one side, and the mint and moneyer's name on the other.

Edgar often came hunting in Devon. He tried to settle the problem of wolves in the woods by accepting 300 wolves' heads instead of cattle for the annual tribute. Edward's half-brother Aethelred tried to settle the Danish problem. Raids had intensified in the 980s.

11 This silver penny of 'long cross' type was issued by the moneyer Wulfsige of Exeter in the reign of Aethelred the Unready between 997 and 1003.

Payments of danegeld were siphoning off hundreds of the new pennies. Aethelred asked the Norman ports not to harbour the raiders, and took Emma of Normandy as his wife, and—after devastating raids in 1001—ordered all the Danes in England to be slaughtered on St Brice's Day, 13 November 1002. King Swein's sister was among them. Swein came rowing up the Exe in 1003 to take revenge on the favourite town of the Saxon kings. Emma held Exeter as a dowry, the 'morning-gift' made after the wedding-night. (This began the tradition of making each royal bride the lady paramount of Exeter.) Emma had installed a Norman bailiff, Hugh, to collect her revenues. He opened the gate to Swein and his men, enabling them to destroy the town and burn down the abbey and its library. When Swein's younger son, Cnut, became king of England in 1016, he married the widowed Emma, rebuilt Exeter's walls, houses and churches, and made the town once more prosperous and secure. The Exeter mint was the fifth or sixth largest in England in his time. Most of the buildings were timber and cob, with thatched roofs. The churches were stone-built, but little of the original fabric can be seen today. The tower of St Olave's, now enclosed by the later aisle, may have been part of the 11th-century church, and some of the original blocks of volcanic stone from Northernhay can be seen reused in its outer walls. St George's stood on the west side of South Street until 1843, when

it was cut away for road-widening. After the Second World War, a remaining Saxon arch was moved across the road, where it stands in the ruined hall of the Vicars Choral. St Martin's proclaims a consecration date of 1065, but this may be the date of the reconsecration of an earlier foundation. There is Saxon work in the crypt of St Stephen's.

In the early 11th century, royal protection was given to four national highways, of which one was the Icknield Way leading to Exeter. The Lammas (Lady Mass) fair was already being held each year on Exe Island at the beginning of August.

In 1050 Bishop Leofric obtained permission from the pope to move his seat from Crediton to the walled city. His personal friend, King Edward the Confessor, took him by the hand, with the queen on the other side, and led him into his cathedral, the abbey church. Edward dispatched the monks to the new abbey he was building at Westminster. Exeter Cathedral was therefore never a monastic foundation and would not be affected by the dissolution of the monasteries. It is still organised according to the charter of 1050 and is thus the oldest surviving institution in the land, centuries older than the United Kingdom itself.

The bishop's charter was witnessed by several members of a powerful local family. Godwin had married a kinswoman of Cnut called Gytha, and had been made Earl of Wessex by Cnut. One of their sons, Harold, was to succeed Edward in January 1065-6. They had also forced Edward to contract a nominal marriage with their daughter Edith in 1045. All these individuals, and Harold's brother Tostig, were among the witnesses named in 1050.

The area vacated by the British in 928 had become known as 'the earl's *burh*'. Godwin had a mansion there. Gytha may have lived there in her widowhood (1053-66). Her daughter the queen was dismissed by King Edward, but continued to hold the royal estate of Wonford.

Saxons had displaced the British, but they themselves were soon to yield precedence to the Normans.

Chapter 3

Castles and Cathedrals

Exeter was a centre of Saxon opposition to the Norman Conquest. King Harold's sister, Queen Edith, still held the royal estate of Wonford. Their widowed mother Gytha took refuge in the town-house of the earls of Wessex. Harold's sons were gathering support in Devon and Cornwall. William led 500 horsemen westwards in late autumn 1068 to demand allegiance from Exeter. A delegation met him four miles outside the city: they agreed to a compromise, and gave hostages. The two parties then progressed to the gates, only to find that the citizens refused to open up until they were assured that the city's tribute would remain unchanged at £18 (£12 to the queen, £6 to the bailiff), payable only when London,

12 King William, a mosaic portrait by Elaine M. Goodwin in the multi-storey car-park on the site of the Norman siege of Eastgate.

13 The gatehouse of Rougemont Castle built for William in 1068 has the oldest military Norman arch in England. Long-and-short stonework and triangular window-heads probably indicate that Saxon masons were employed. The entrance was fitted with a drawbridge over a ditch. The adjacent modern gateway dates from the 1770s when the castle was rebuilt and the approach was realigned.

York and Winchester were taxed. William, furious, had a hostage blinded in front of them, but the citizens remained adamant. The Normans laid siege to the city, mined under the east gate and camped outside, growing impatient as the weather became wintry. After 18 days part of the wall collapsed and the citizens agreed on a conditional surrender. William swore on the cathedral's holy relics that he would leave Exeter's tax status unchanged. Gytha was allowed to depart. But the king would not be defied again: he would plant a castle inside the walls, towering over the rest of the town, on the red hill called *rouge mont* in Norman French. William created his friend Baldwin sheriff of Devon, with responsibility for building and manning the castle (and one at Okehampton). Forty-eight houses (a tenth of the housing stock) were demolished to make way for Rougemont Castle and its sprawling earthworks. The massive ditch is still a feature of Rougemont Gardens. The steep slope above Gandy Street by the Arts Centre is a remnant of the outer earth-bank.

William confiscated the earl's estate in the north-west quarter (including Gytha's church of St Olaf) and gave it to the Benedictine monks of the Abbey of St Martin which he had founded in Battle. They set up a priory, dedicating its church in 1087 to the fourth-century bishop Nicholas, whose bones were moved in that year to Bari in the Norman kingdom of Sicily.

In the disputed succession of 1136, the citizens were loyal to King Stephen, but the Earl Baldwin of the time held the castle for his own cousin Matilda. Baldwin's wife and children were with him, protected by a garrison of 'valiant youths in shining armour'. Stephen's men besieged Rougemont for three months, attacking with fire and stones, arrows and tunnels, even building a temporary castle of their own on the opposite bank of the Longbrook. (This castle has been visible again since 1992, when 'Danes' Castle' reservoir was moved, and the earthwork which it had concealed since 1852 was identified as a temporary Norman defence.) Baldwin's men sallied out to slay with the sword, or they sent showers of arrows over the walls. Stephen's men retaliated with battering-rams and wooden siege-towers. Baldwin's men held firm

when the castle wells ran dry, but then the wine ran out—and they surrendered.

Meanwhile, a new cathedral was rising in shiny milky-white stone. William Warelwast, a nephew of the Conqueror, became Exeter's third bishop in 1107. Tithes from the recently-discovered rich veins of tin near Tavistock helped to finance the grand Romanesque church which replaced the Saxon minster. The new high altar was consecrated in 1133 but the building was not completed until the end of the century, five bishops later. By then the city also had more than thirty little churches and chapels, served by a streetful of priests, Preston Street.

Before 1160 there was a leper hospital, for not more than 13 sufferers, at a hygienic distance from the south gate, on the further

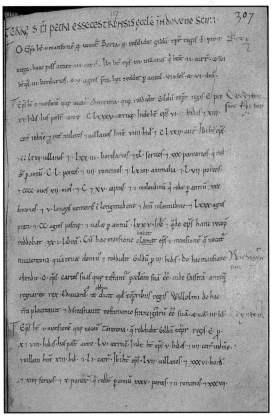

14 *Exeter Domesday* is the draft of the returns for the south-west counties. This page lists the lands of St Peter's church in Exeter in Devonshire, i.e. of the cathedral, held by bishop O(sbern) (1073-1103), who was one of the Domesday commissioners. His income from this large diocese made him the sixth wealthiest bishop in England.

Exeter St Nicholas Priory The Crypt

15 The 11th-century undercroft of St Nicholas' Priory.

16 Bishop Warelwast's new cathedral took most of the 12th century to build. Square towers like castle keeps, decorated with arcading, were set north and south of the nave.

17   The Norman font of St Mary Steps.

18   The church of St Mary Arches was enlarged in the late 12th century and still has its Norman pillars.

19 An impression of the silver Common Seal of the City of Exeter which uses the image of the new Norman cathedral and probably dates from about 1200. It is the earliest civic seal in England (although the cathedral chapter were using one with a similar, but simpler, design half a century before).

bank of the southern brook. Dedicated to St Mary Magdalene, its name lives on in the street which led there.

In 1154 William of Malmesbury wrote of Exeter: 'By reason of its stateliness, the wealth of its citizens, and the great resort of strangers, it so abounds with all sorts of merchandise, that nothing is wanting that can be reckoned useful'.

In 1189 Richard Lionheart granted a charter to the city releasing the merchants from certain taxes. From 1191 the city paid the royal dowry to the Lionheart's queen, Berengaria, lady paramount of Exeter. It also paid a large sum towards Richard's ransom when he was captured on his way back from the Holy Land. He had been attended on the outward journey by Joseph, the Swan of Isca, 'the miracle of his age in classical composition', who was inspired by his travels to write epics in Latin about wars ancient and modern, *De bello Antiocheno* and *De bello Troiano*.

Exeter's river was wide, and usually shallow enough to ford on horseback. Foot-travellers could use a rather shaky bridge made of 'clappers of tymbre'. Nicholas Gervase, a prominent citizen and mill-owner, proposed to rebuild it in stone. His son collected funds

from near and far. Soon after 1200 (once a hermitess had been been dislodged from her cell which had blocked the new bridge for five years) travellers could pass safely over the stream and its marshy banks.

By then, woollen cloth was being made on a commercial scale, processed in fulling-mills driven by the Exe. Exeter now had a mayor, the earliest after London and Winchester. In 1217 the nine-year-old Henry III came to the throne, and asked Robert Courtenay, whose family now held Rougemont, to vacate one chamber and the great hall for the use of the dowager queen. Two years later he had to repeat the request. In 1228, fully grown, Henry gave the revenues from Exeter to his brother Richard, Earl of Cornwall, later Holy Roman Emperor. From that date, the castle was traditionally assigned to the earls of Cornwall. Earl Richard was a friend and patron of the Franciscans at Oxford. Soon after the death of St Francis in 1226, a little group of eight came to Exeter, perhaps encouraged by Richard. They settled behind St Nicholas' Priory, living in poverty and caring for the poor and sick. They were known as grey friars from the colour of their cloaks. The street which led to their first house is still called Friernhay.

On the opposite side of town, in the south-east quarter, Bishop Brewer established a priory for the followers of Francis' friend Dominic, known as black friars. In September 1232 the king gave them permission to quarry stone for a church from the side of Rougemont, from a spot where it would not undermine the castle.

William Brewer, bishop 1224-44, was away from 1227 to 1235, leading crusaders to the Holy Land, and then escorting the king's sister Isabella to Germany to marry Emperor Frederick II. Before he set out, he appointed Serlo to the new office of dean. When Brewer came home, he may have brought drawings of exotic Asian beasts and news of the latest European literature—this would explain the choice of decorations for the cathedral misericords, which are the oldest set surviving in England. The carvings include mermaids, grotesques, an elephant, foliage and parrots. There are knights in 13th-century surcoats, chain-mail and flat-top helmets, acting out scenes from Arthurian romances, including Lohengrin in a boat pulled by a swan.

20 Arches from the 13th-century Exebridge now cross dry land. In the middle ages houses perched on the sides of the bridge, and a weir lay just downstream. A visitor in 1635 saw 'a fair stone bridge of 20 arches, under which the dainty Salmon Trouts come trolling'. Celia Fiennes in 1695 saw salmon being speared as they leapt the weir.

21 Part of an effigy of a knight in chain-mail, found on the site of the Dominican monastery. The black friars' church was dedicated to St Katherine in November 1259. They occupied a large site east of the Close for about 500 years.

By this time, Exeter had a water-supply running through underground tunnels, possibly drawing from the same springs as the Romans had done. Frontinus, author of a handbook on hydraulic engineering and aqueducts, was governor of Britain in A.D. 74-7, and it was he who ordered the Second Augustan legion to move from Exeter to Caerleon. A generation later, the Roman town was bringing water from outside Eastgate, round the north side of Rougemont, to cross the town-ditch near present-day Maddocks Row, in a wooden aqueduct datable to A.D. 101. During the following centuries an Iscan engineer may have devised a shorter route, maintaining the necessary downhill gradient by tunnelling a short distance under the hump by the east gate. When the new cathedral was begun in the 12th century, it was sited to the east of the Saxon church. The work blocked the spring used by the bishop's household, and once again water had to be brought in from the eastern ridge. The first written references to the underground passages constructed for this purpose date from 1226. The supply was divided between the cathedral staff, the monks of St Nicholas, and the townsfolk. At first the water ran along the floor of the tunnels, then in 1347 lead piping was laid and the passages were made large enough for maintenance men to walk along. In 1420 the city Chamber (as the governing body was called until 1835) built its own separate system. Today the complex network of burrows provides a fascinating tourist attraction under the east gate.

From 1228 to 1230 it rained nonstop. In 1234 plague swept through England, and more than two-thirds of Exeter's population died.

In 1270 Bishop Bronescombe began to rebuild the eastern end of the cathedral to accommodate liturgical changes. Once the modernisation was started it seemed to acquire its own momentum: it was continued by succeeding bishops until only the two towers remained from the Norman building. The nave was extended in one unbroken avenue of slender, soaring, branching, clustered pillars, clasped by jewel-like bosses where they met far overhead.

In 1276 the Lammas Fair was moved from Exe Island to Southernhay (then called Crulditch). Many foreign merchants thronged to this event. Part of the city walls stood between noisy Crulditch and the cathedral, preserving the peaceful seclusion of the bishop's grounds. The other sides of the cathedral yard were surrounded only by a low wall. Criminals sometimes jumped into the consecrated ground to avoid arrest. In November 1283 there was a serious incident. Walter de Lechlade, the cathedral precentor, was attacked and killed as he walked the short distance from a night-time service to his lodgings in the chantry. Various cathedral officials and the mayor himself were implicated, and the dispute dragged on. Two years later King Edward I and Queen Eleanor came to spend Christmas with the bishop in order to settle the matter. The king then gave permission for the cathedral yard to be enclosed by a high wall. All access gates would be locked at night.

It is thought that before the 1280s the main street curved north, round the sprawling burial-ground, then ran south of St Petrock's and down Smythen Street and Stepcote Hill to the west gate and Exebridge. The new cathedral defences ran through the sites of the present-day *Royal Clarence Hotel*, old Tinley's and St Petrock's, displacing the High Street to its present line, and moving the Carfax to its present position at the junction with Fore Street, North Street and South Street. The town conduit was also resited.

In 1287 the Franciscans were allowed to move from the increasingly unhygienic site behind St Nicholas' Priory to the airy height above the quay, still called Friar's Walk. They dedicated their church there to St John the Baptist.

Exeter has many claims to fame: first mention of an English theatre, first pound-lock canal in England, first shilling-in-the-slot gas-meter. Trainee town-planners are taught that the first planning appeal was Exeter's complaint to the crown that the Countess of Devon had 'made a great nuisance by erecting a weare ...; salmon fishing is now destroyed on this side. Boats and vessels laden with wine and merchandise cannot come up'. The document survives from 1461. In the 1290s Countess Isabella, who owned land on both sides of the estuary, had built weirs for her mills, leaving only a small gap in midstream. Her successor completed the blockage. For centuries Exeter's loss was Topsham's gain. Ships had to unload

22 *Above left.* St Katherine's Priory at Polsloe was the only house for Benedictine nuns in the diocese. It was founded before 1160 and rebuilt *c.*1300. In January 1320 the bishop had to remind the sisters to speak more softly, to use Latin, to come to services and meals promptly, and not to have so many visitors through this gate.

23 *Above right.* The towers retained from the Norman cathedral stand outside the 14th-century nave, allowing it to become the longest uninterrupted Gothic vault in Christendom.

at Topsham quay and pay dues there. But the Courtenays continually fell into royal disfavour; the city made haste each time to petition the sovereign to restore access to Exeter quay—but to no avail for 250 years.

In 1307 Edward II appointed his childhood friend the frivolous Piers Gaveston as Earl of Cornwall and Lord of Exeter. Edward III raised the earldom to a duchy (also the first in England), granted it to the Black Prince, and enhanced Exeter's value by adding to it the manor of Bradninch. Exeter's castle began to be regarded as the manor-house of Bradninch, giving its surroundings the title 'Precinct of Bradninch'.

Around 1300 Wonford manor became the property of the Montacute family. In 1345 William de Montacute married the sister of Bishop Grandisson. She it was whose fallen garter was picked up by Edward III, who allegedly said, 'Honi soit qui mal y pense' and made it the motto of the Order of the Garter, founded in 1348. French was still the language of the royal court.

In 1348 and 1352 Bishop Grandisson instructed his archdeacon to ban a 'sect of malign men' who were mocking the leather-dressers in the theatre at Exeter. Apparently the leather-dressers had been overcharging, but public satire might provoke a riot.

24 *Above left.* The many daily masses sung in the chapels of the new cathedral required a back-up team of vicars choral. In 1387 a college was built for them behind the deanery, in Kalenderhay. It had a strong gatehouse, a row of little houses left and right (one for each member) and a common kitchen and dining-hall at the far end.

25 *Above right.* The hall of the Vicars Choral had no doorway onto South Street while it served their college.

In the years of the Black Death (1349-51), Exeter was one of the worst-hit areas, losing half of its population, and then a quarter of the survivors when the plague returned after 13 years. Clergy visiting the sick and burying the dead succumbed one after the other. Bishop Grandisson was given papal permission to ordain 100 replacements, but he was unable to find enough candidates. Nevertheless, religious and commercial life continued. In 1353 Exeter was recognised as one of the main markets for wool, leather skins and lead. Also in 1353, the minstrels' gallery in the cathedral,

decorated with angel musicians, was finished in time for the Palm Sunday procession. By 1369 the cathedral was declared complete. The west front was exposed to view, with ranks of angels, saints and prophets, carved in stone and painted in red and green, yellow and white.

The cathedral had a simple timepiece as early as 1284. The Fabric Accounts of 1327 and 1376 refer to it as the *horologium qui vocatur clokke*. Here an English word bobs up, an assurance that Anglo-Saxon was still the language of the street, whatever was being spoken in the castle and the bishop's palace.

Chapter 4

Carpenters and Kings

In 1403 Henry IV greeted his second bride, Joan of Navarre, at Falmouth, and brought her to Exeter for two nights on the way to their wedding at Winchester. As they approached Exeter from the west they would have seen the white cathedral towering over the low, tightly-packed houses on the city's slopes. A few thatched houses stood beside the approach roads, but at this time (and for the next 400 years) market gardens and orchards encircled the city. There were still wooded hills all around, but also many fields of pasture, grazed by the vast numbers of sheep kept for their wool. There were also large green

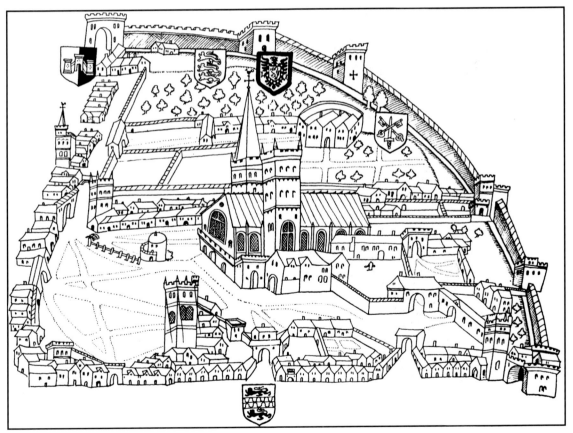

26 This drawing, based on a map in Hooker's *History of Exeter* (1587), shows the city walls from Eastgate to Southgate, the gates to the cathedral close, and the large area between the cathedral and Eastgate occupied by the Dominicans.

21

27 Wynard's Hospital was built in 1435. In the Civil War it was used as a fortification and damaged. It was restored in 1863 but this did not spoil the serenity of its red stone walls, cobbled courtyard and cool chapel.

28 These may be the two houses 'north of St Martin's Church' which a mason contracted to build in 1404 for £6 6s. 8d. He did a good job: they still enhance the corner of Cathedral Yard.

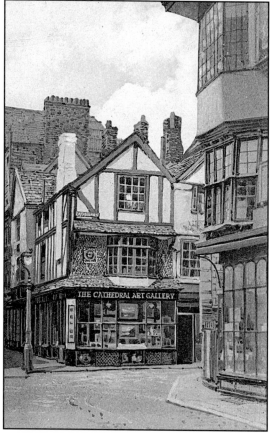

areas within the walls: the enclosed castle grounds, the cathedral yard, the Dominicans' domain and the land of St Nicholas' Priory. The townsfolk were crammed into the remaining space, merchants living above their shops along the main streets, artisans in cottages, mainly in the west quarter where the land falls away to the river.

The 15th century saw a building boom. Red sandstone quarried at Heavitree was near at hand and easily worked. Many cartloads rumbled in as the city's churches were enlarged or completely rebuilt, almshouses were founded, splendid halls were raised by corporate bodies and merchants' premises were upgraded. In 1435 William Wynard endowed a hospice on Magdalen Road for 12 infirm paupers and a priest. Wynard owned the *White Hart Inn* in South Street, sagging a little now but still a credit to its builders.

7 EXETER. — S^t. Catherine's Alms Houses.

29 By the will of Canon John Stevens (1457), St Catherine's almshouses also sheltered a dozen of the poor and infirm. They were each allotted a tiny room. In the middle there was a small chapel with a common chamber above it. Egypt Lane ran alongside the almshouses.

30 In 1285-6 the cathedral yard was walled off from the town, following the murder of the precentor one dark night. Access was through gates at St Martin's, St Petrock's, St George's, the Deanery, the Palace and (here) Broadgate, also called St Michael's.

31 This is a plate from an early 'hornbook' mislaid *c*.1500, and untypically made of copper alloy. Saracen dress was fashionable in the later 15th century. Children learnt their letters from the alphabet in upper and lower case at the top, then 'a' stands beside the archer.

Henry VI and Queen Margaret toured their troubled realm in 1452. They were met at Clyst Honiton on 16 July by the nobles and gentlemen of Devon, then by the Exeter civic party, numbering 300, all in mulberry-red gowns and black velvet capes, with the shoulders embroidered with the city's arms: a castle triple-towered. The clergy and friars awaited the king at Livery Dole, then joined the procession as it continued to the south gate, where the high cross was 'gorgeously apparelled'. Old Bishop Lacy, who had been at Agincourt, waited at the Broadgate, where the king dismounted. The Carfax conduit ran with wine (achieved by inserting a hogshead of claret behind the spout). The king's son was not yet even conceived, so the king himself was both sovereign and seigneur of Exeter. (Ten years earlier he had appointed an Exeter man as clerk of works for his new foundation of Eton College. This may explain why Eton Chapel had a wall-painting of Exeter's St Sidwell.)

In 1457 the east gate suddenly collapsed one midday, with no loss of life, but it had to be rebuilt in those uncertain times. In 1466 the city's muddy streets and alleys were paved with stone after a gap of a thousand years. A remarkable series of elaborate timbered hall-roofs survive from this century. The arch-braced roofs of Bowhill are two of them. The Law Library at 8 Cathedral Close has a roof with hammer beams ending in horizontal angel figures: it is comparable in beauty and quality to the roof of Westminster Hall made in 1399. Bishop Lacy began building a chapter house before the middle of the century, and Bishop Bothe had it raised higher under an ornate beamed ceiling in 1470.

Exeter had long prided itself on its loyalty to the crown, but during the Wars of the Roses it was no simple matter for the mayor to welcome the right party. The rival factions of York and Lancaster were fighting bloody battles. The main figures suddenly changed sides, or were murdered, or slain in the fighting. In 1453 King Henry became mentally ill and the Duke of York seized control. In 1459 the Earl of Warwick fled to Exeter with York's son (the future King Edward IV). Warwick's brothers were in positions of power here: one was Marquis of Montacute, and the other was the new young bishop, George Neville. However, the townsfolk were loyal to the crowned king, Henry, and Warwick found it advisable to lie low at Nutwell, on the estuary, and then set sail from Lympstone to France. In 1461 he returned with Edward to proclaim him King, Prince of Wales, Duke of Cornwall and Lord of Exeter. The Guildhall accounts for 1468-70 survive only in part, but it is thought that the elaborate timbered roof was built at this time. At first glance the carved supporters seem to be the bear and ragged staff of Warwick's insignia, but a closer look reveals a monkey and staff, a dog and staff, and so on. Could it be deliberate mockery of the turncoat Warwick? By 1469 Warwick had switched allegiance to Henry's queen and young prince, another Edward, and had married one of his daughters to the Duke of Clarence, the disloyal brother of King Edward. In the spring of 1470 Henry's party was on the run. The Duchess of Clarence took refuge in the bishop's palace, and a thousand of his followers found lodgings with the canons. Bishop Bothe fled. King Edward's local adherents, led by Sir William Courtenay, began a siege of the city on 16 March, breaking down the bridges and cutting off much-needed supplies of food. No markets could be held for 12 days: there was a real danger of famine. The supporters of the white rose and of the red rose each asked the mayor to hand over the keys of the city, but he refused. He said he would yield them only to the king,

32 Bowhill stands above the flood plain on the western slopes facing the city. It was built in the 15th century for the Holland family, who supplied Exeter's member of parliament for three generations. In 1488 the Holland heiress married a Carew; it was possibly then that the fine arch-braced roof was added to the great hall in this southern range.

33 The town hall was called the *Gihalde*, meaning simply 'Guild', from the 12th century until the 15th, since when it has been called Guildhall. It has always been used as a court room; there are prison cells at the rear.

34 Bishop Peter Courtenay is thought to have had this dial fitted to the cathedral clock in 1484. It shows the earth in the centre, the moon revolving round it (and turning to show its phases) and a fleur-de-lys sun circling the earth every 24 hours while also pointing to the day of the lunar month.

since the city yielded revenue only to the king; but 'certain canons of the cathedral' mediated between the parties and the siege was raised. Three weeks later, on 3 April, Warwick and the Duke of Clarence came fleeing south (chased by King Edward and 10,000 men) and joined the party in the palace while they hastily arranged evacuation by ship from Dartmouth. The king arrived on the 14th, 'but the birds had flown'. The mayor handed him the keys and a purse containing 100 gold nobles. The king rested with his men for three days, including Palm Sunday, when he joined in the procession, then they all set out for London. By September, Warwick had married his other daughter to the young prince, Edward. He came back to Devon, raised 60,000 men, and reinstated Henry as king in October. Edward IV fled to Holland, but in spring 1471 he came back, Clarence returned to his side, and on 13 April they slew Warwick at the battle of Barnet. On the same day, Henry's queen, Margaret, and Prince Edward landed at Weymouth, came to lodge with the Black Friars at Exeter, and raised another army. They were defeated on 4 May at Tewkesbury. Prince Edward was killed. On 21 May King Henry was murdered in the Tower of London. Edward IV was king again.

While the dynasties clashed, and sudden tides of armed men swept through Exeter, the city's merchants minded their own business. Several trades guilds gained charters of incorporation at the end of this century and the beginning of the next. The wealthy Guild of Weavers, Tuckers and Shearmen, who controlled the main local industry, the flourishing woollen trade, built themselves a grand stone meeting-place in 1471. The hall, which has a fine wagon roof, can still be visited in Fore Street. The barbers and cappers each had a guild, and the butchers and brewers, bakers and cordwainers, glovers and skinners, smiths and cutlers. A trade supplied a living and often a surname too, as the skills and 'tools of the trade' were handed down in the family.

From September 1479 to the end of November 1480 'incredible numbers' of people were swept away by pestilence in London and in Exeter.

When King Edward died in 1483, Richard of York allegedly had the young heirs killed in the Tower, had himself crowned in York, and came to Devon to stamp out local hostility. The king was challenged, as Shakespeare says in *Richard III*, by 'Sir Edward Courtenay, and the haughty prelate, / Bishop of Exeter, his elder brother, / With many more confederates in arms'.

The king was greeted by the mayor at the east gate and given a purse of 200 gold nobles. He lodged in the palace. Bishop Courtenay had fled. He and his brothers were declared outlaws. At the trial of conspirators in Torrington, two gentlemen were found guilty of high treason. One was the king's own brother-in-law, Sir Thomas Leger. They were

brought to the Carfax in Exeter to be beheaded by the sword.

In 1485 Richard was killed at the battle of Bosworth, and Henry Earl of Richmond was crowned as Henry VII. Shakespeare used an anecdote about Exeter in *Richard III*. The king had once been told that he would die soon after he saw Richmond. When the mayor was showing him round Exeter in 1483, he mentioned that the castle was called Rougemont. The king heard it as Richmond, 'whereat he fell into a great dump'.

Under Henry VII the Courtenays were back in favour. Bishop Peter Courtenay could return to his palace. In an unusual gesture, the Earl of Devon, Sir Edward Courtenay, was made a freeeman of the city. His son Sir William had married a daughter of Edward IV, Katherine Plantagenet. In 1496 some pleasant jobs were available: 'Aletasters were apoynted for serching that holsome Drynke shold be made'.

In 1497 the city suffered two assaults. 16,000 Cornishmen marching to protest against a 'subsidie' demanded by the crown were denied entry. When the mayor found no support forthcoming from the lords of the shire, he grudgingly allowed the angry captains to pass through, but their men had to go

35 The Bishop's Palace has been altered many times since it began as a 13th-century hall. Bishop Courtenay installed a magnificent carved stone fireplace in 1486. Bishop Phillpotts added the bay window to the palace in 1845. It came from Elyot's House, which stood behind the *Globe Inn* and near St Petrock's church.

36 The mayoral party of 1905, displaying the sword and cap of maintenance granted to the city in 1497 to be carried in front of the mayor on all official occasions.

grumbling round the outside of the walls and rejoin them at Eastgate. An explosive situation was defused.

Soon afterwards, a smaller band collected at Bodmin when Perkin Warbeck arrived there in pursuit of his claim to be the younger of the 'princes in the Tower'. He reached Exeter on 17 September with an army of four or five thousand and found the gates shut against them, but this time the Courtenays were inside, lodging with the Black Friars, ready to help defend the city, having been reprimanded for not turning up the last time. Warbeck's men tried to burn down the north gate but found their losses were too great there, where the defenders were safely inside and on higher ground. They moved to the flatter approaches of the east gate and managed to break it open, and started fighting their way towards the castle, but the Courtenays, father and son, came rushing out with their men, there was furious fighting on the High Street, and Warbeck's band withdrew, to make for Taunton. Meeting the king, Warbeck surrendered to him, and was brought back through the east gate as a prisoner on 7 October.

The king lodged at the treasurer's house, which abutted the north tower of the cathedral. (The marks of its gable can still be seen.) Warbeck was sent to the Tower of London. The other leaders were condemned to be hanged and quartered on Southernhay Green. The rest were brought before the king's window with nooses around their necks. The window had been enlarged for the occasion, and several trees had been felled to clear the view. The men begged for pardon, swore to be loyal in future, and were released. That year there had also been trouble over deciding on a mayor. The king laid down election rules, imposed his own choice of mayor for that year, 'and to encourage the mayor and citizens to continue dutiful and obedient subjects as tofore, he took his sword which he then wore about his middle, and gave it to the mayor together with a "hatt of mayntenunce", to be borne before him and his successors, as it is used in the Citie of London'. The city's right to bear a sword has been proudly exercised ever since, a symbol of loyalty to the crown and a reminder of times when men lived and died by the sword.

Chapter 5

Reformation and Resistance

An incident in 1501 presaged the turbulent times still to come. The bishop had negotiated a marriage between the king's eldest son, Prince of Wales, Lord of Exeter, and the 15-year-old Spanish Infanta. Escorting her on a long and stormy journey to what would be two marriages, a short one ending in widowhood, then a long one ending in divorce, he lodged the royal party at the deanery. 'The weather was very foul and windy ... the weathercock upon the Church of St Mary the More ... did so whistle that the princess could not sleep'. A workman braved the wind and dark to climb the steeple and take down the squeaking weathercock on St Mary Major which was disturbing young Catherine of Aragon.

37 The deanery hall was given an oak roof of arch-braced trusses springing from stone corbels.

38 Eastgate had been broken down by Perkin Warbeck's men. In 1511 it was rebuilt more strongly, with two solid bulwarks flanking a curtain wall, adorned on its outer face with a figure of Henry VII in a Roman toga. Eastgate was taken down in 1784. After the Second World War a figure of Henry VII in armour was put up nearby.

39 This house was built at the corner of Edmund Street and Frog Street c.1500, with a west wall of Heavitree stone, and a timber frame filled with mud and wattle. The projecting upper storeys are supported by triple-headed corner posts. In December 1961 the house was dragged 50 yards uphill to make way for a new road.

In 1511 Sir William Courtenay died of pleurisy, and his young widow, the Countess Katharine (who was proud of being daughter, sister and aunt of kings), retired to Devon to live off her estates, including Columbjohn near Exeter. Her household accounts for 1523-4 reveal some local supplies (cream, apples for pies, eels) but also many luxuries imported via Topsham and Exeter: sour and sweet oranges, licorice, caraways, rices, figs, ginger, cloves, sugar loaf, cherries; velvet, satin, linen, furs... She was obviously fond of marmalade. Hull of Exeter had sent her a box of it the previous year (and the recipe?). This predates the earliest use of the word *marmalade* cited in the *Oxford English Dictionary*: a letter mentioning a box of it sent to Henry VIII in 1524 by (presumably the same) Hull of Exeter.

The religious upheavals of the Reformation rocked the West Country. A Master of Arts from Cambridge, Thomas Benet, came to Exeter in 1525 and ran a small school in Smythen Street. In 1531 he began pinning placards to the cathedral door proclaiming such Lutheran sentiments as 'We ought to worship God only and no saints'. He was condemned to be burnt as a heretic. The mayor refused the use of Southernhay, Benet refused to retract his beliefs, and he died at the stake at Livery Dole on 15 January 1532. By this time Henry VIII was already in the process of breaking with Rome. He soon sent Bishop Hugh Latimer on a tour to preach the Reformation. Latimer reached Exeter in June 1534. First he spoke to a crowd in the churchyard of the Greyfriars outside Southgate. They were undeterred when it began to rain. As he continued to preach very earnestly his nose began to bleed, which the friars took as a sign of God's displeasure, but their own warden, John Cardemaker, was won over (to the extent that, like Latimer himself, he would be burnt in 1555, after Queen Mary had restored the supremacy of Rome). Latimer also preached

40 As part of the dissolution of the monasteries the 13 nuns in St Katherine's Priory were pensioned off in 1538. The surviving western range, containing guest-rooms, prioress's chamber and priest's accommodation, became a manor-house, then a farmhouse, more recently a council store, and now a community hall, with a unique 14th-century oaken screen and corbel heads.

in St Mary Major, although the clergy complained that it would interfere with the celebration of their feast day. Such a great crowd gathered in and around the church that its windows were broken to allow those outside to hear, and one Thomas Carew Esquire heckled loudly and called Latimer to come down from the pulpit or he would pull him by the ears.

In 1535 the king sent commissioners to dissolve the smaller monasteries. In Exeter they began by viewing St Nicholas' Priory, then retired for dinner, after ordering a workman to pull down the rood loft. But the priory's tenants rushed to defend it. They depended on a distribution every Friday of a twopenny loaf, a pottle of ale, a piece of fish and a penny in money. A number of women came running with shovels and pikes and sticks. They broke open the church door and chased the workman up the tower. He jumped out of a window, breaking a rib. Somebody fetched Alderman Blackaller to pacify the women, but Elizabeth Glandfield 'gave him a blow and sent him packing'. The women barricaded themselves in the church, until the mayor came and arrested them and allowed the commissioners to continue their work. By 1539 the priory's church and cloister had been demolished. Some of the stone was bought for the mayor's new project, a hall for a weekly yarn market, to rival one at Crediton. Other loads of the stone were used to repair Exebridge, where a central arch had collapsed one night, together with the dwelling house on it, so that its tenants, John Cove and his wife, found themselves floating down the Exe on their bed.

41 Similarly, the surviving western range of St Nicholas' Priory contains the guest-hall, kitchen, chambers and main entrance. An alley now divides it from the surviving north side of the cloisters, where the monks ate and slept.

In 1537 Henry VIII granted Exeter a charter making it an independent county separate from Devonshire. It could elect its own sheriff. An Act of 1550 clarified the boundaries. The extramural parishes of St David's and St Sidwell's were included, but the castle and its precincts were not. On 6 August 1564 the city's arms were confirmed as the 'castle triple-towered' with the addition of supporters in the form of two winged horses (although the College of Arms cannot have known that Pegasus was the insignia of the Second Augustan legion, or that this legion founded Exeter). The citizens were proud to use the description 'city and county of the city of Exeter' until they lost the privilege in the 1972 reorganisation of local government.

A Dominican, the Bishop of Dover, was appointed to dissolve the Exeter friaries. The Greyfriars' site, with 300 elms, was subsequently leased to a member of the family of marmalade importers, John Hull, who lived at neighbouring Larkbeare. The Dominican house, with church, belfry and churchyard, was included in a large grant from the king to Lord John Russell, who was overseeing the reformation in the West. Russell used it as a residence and called it Bedford House.

The Courtenays suffered a great fall from grace. Henry Courtenay had been a favourite of the king. He had even been named as heir to the throne before Henry VIII had any children of his own. But in 1538 he was accused of treason, and was executed the following January. His possessions reverted to the crown. This time the city's long-standing complaint was heeded. An Act of Parliament of 1539 authorised the clearing of obstructions from the river. However, the Courtenay weirs proved too solid to uproot. They would have to be bypassed with a canal. Work began in 1545. Silver plate was collected from the city's parish churches towards the great expense. Francis Drake suggested enlarging the mill-leat at Countess Wear which ran a straight course along the eastern bank. Little progress was made until the engineer John Trew was engaged in 1563. His workmen found themselves cutting through solid rock. Trew therefore proposed routing 'the new haven' through the softer ground west of the stream. Work began again in 1564. By 1566 ships were able to pass to Exeter quay, through seven sluices,

42 Sir Edward Courtenay (1526-56). After his father's execution he spent 14 years of his boyhood in the Tower of London, where he is said to have carved the words *Ubi lapsus? quid feci?* The death of Edward VI saved this Courtenay from the block. Queen Mary created him Earl of Devon.

six of them paired, making this the first pound-lock canal in England. A new stone quay was constructed below the city walls, furnished with a crane.

Meanwhile, the religious turmoil continued. Edward VI, coming to the throne in 1547, ordered all the images of saints to be removed from the churches. The Latin mass-book was to be replaced by the *English Book of Common Prayer*, the change-over to be completed by Whitsunday 1549. The Cornish particularly resented the innovation because it imposed the English language on them. As they set out to march to London to protest they were joined by crowds of Devon churchgoers who also loved their familiar form of Latin service. The demonstrators reached Exeter on 2 July 1549, in a solemn procession headed by

43 The hall of the Vicars Choral was fitted with linenfold oak panelling in the 16th century. A visitor in 1635 found there 'a Cup of good Ale, wch I liberally tasted off, with their honest Organist, and some of the merry Vicars ...'.

priests and a banner portraying the five wounds of Christ. The rebels had formulated their demands: 'We will not receive the new Service because it is but like a Christmas game. We will have every priest in his mass pray specially by name for the souls in Purgatory as our forefathers did ...'. They hoped to find support and supplies in Exeter, but the gates were shut against them. They laid siege instead, and tried to burn down the gates. One hot-head even proposed burning down the city by firing redhot shot onto the houses in North Street. The vicar of St Thomas, Robert Welshe, persuaded him that this would benefit nobody. Welshe was a Cornishman himself, and sympathised with the rebels, but he tried to moderate their violence. They had captured St Sidwell's church, as it lay outside the walls, and they held prisoners in its tower, including

Sir Walter Raleigh senior, who had told off an old woman for carrying a rosary. Inside the town, the citizens were reduced to eating horse-meat and then the redundant horse-fodder. They were relieved after five weeks by Lord John Russell. He sent most of the surviving rebels home to Cornwall, but made an example of the ring-leaders. Robert Welshe was condemned as a traitor. The execution was turned into a lesson in political correct-ness, for he was hung from his own church tower in his Roman vestments, carrying a rosary 'and other Popish trash'.

Russell's chaplain during this campaign was Miles Coverdale, who had made the English translation of the whole Bible which Henry VIII had ordered in 1538 to be set up and used in every church. In 1551 Coverdale became bishop of Exeter. He was preaching

44 Nicholas Hilliard (1547-1619) was
born in Exeter, son of a goldsmith, was
appointed limner and goldsmith to Queen
Elizabeth I at the age of 24 and became
the first great painter of miniature
portraits. He made this self-portrait in
1577.

45 Thomas Bodley (1545-1613), the
distinguished diplomat, was born in Exeter,
son of a leading citizen, a printer and active
Protestant, who took his family (and the
young Nicholas Hilliard) to Geneva during
Mary's reign. Hilliard painted this miniature
of his fellow-Exonian and friend in 1598,
the year in which Bodley refounded the
library of Oxford University. (Poole Portrait
73.)

in the cathedral in July 1553 when the news came that Mary was queen. He stopped preaching and fled, later leaving the country for the duration of Mary's reign. Other leading Protestants in Exeter also found it prudent to go into voluntary exile. Less courageous people bowed to the prevailing wind. William Horne, parson of the mayor's parish church, St Petrock's, stated publicly during the reign of Edward VI that he would rather be torn with wild horses than say mass again. Seeing him saying a mass as soon as Mary became queen, the mayor reminded him of what he had said. Horne replied in front of the congregation, 'There is no remedy, man'. Welshe's tarred corpse was at last taken down from his church tower after hanging there for four years. Now Protestants suffered again. Agnes Prest denied the doctrine of transubstantiation. Walter Raleigh's mother defiantly visited her in prison. Agnes was burned at the stake in Southernhay in November 1557. She and Thomas Benet are commemorated by a tall obelisk in Denmark

Road. (Exeter was to have a Catholic martyr in 1599 when James Dowdall denied the queen's spiritual supremacy. He was hanged, drawn and quartered at the castle.)

Protestant Elizabeth succeeded Catholic Mary in 1558 and once again there came the command that the (recently replaced) images of saints should be destroyed. By September her emissaries were lodged in the Deanery supervising the stripping of the cathedral of its statues and ornaments, and their destruction on a bonfire in the churchyard. The new individual responsibility for one's soul did not make everyone virtuous immediately, but it led to one odd incident. John Hooker records that the Cathedral exchequer was robbed in 1566, 'but the thieves had such good conscience that when they had carried home the money and found it to be more than they needed, they carried back the overplus'.

During Elizabeth's reign various civic improvements were undertaken. In 1568 the City Chamber chose three sites for 'common jakes'. One was at the Snayle Tower, in the

46 The Guildhall—the oldest municipal building in the country still in use—is documented from 1160, but the solid oak door and distinctive portico were not added until 1593-4. The pillars are of Dartmoor granite. Until the early 19th century drunkards were punished by an hour in the stocks. This drawing is part of a vignette on Roque's map of 1744.

47 Three centuries after the Elizabethan sea captains met here in the first-floor room, 'Mol's Coffee House' had become Worth's Art Gallery. A plain pointed roof-line was replaced in the 1890s with the ornate gable seen here.

steep north-western angle of the walls. In 1575 the mayor, Thomas Prestwood junior, had boundary stones set up at the limits of the city-shire, at Marypole Head, Scarlet's Cross (now Stoke Hill roundabout), at the top of Blackboy Road and so on. (Two hundred years later these would be the sites of the tollgates for the turnpike roads.) Prestwood was a wealthy merchant who had a pair of four-storied houses built in the High Street (now nos. 225-6), with ornate façades. Another tall timber-framed house is a landmark at the corner of the Cathedral close. In the 1590s it was owned by an Italian, Thomas Mol, and the premises were used as a coffee-house from about 1700. The first-floor casement has been compared to the poop of an Elizabethan galleon. The panelled room that it lights is believed to have been the meeting-place of the great Devon 'sea-dogs' Drake, Raleigh, Gilbert, Hawkins and their like. In Exeter they could hear the latest news from Europe brought by returning merchant-ships, or news from London brought by waggoners or the

riders of the Royal Post. Exeter has been called 'Hell for horses', the way being uphill in nearly every direction coming or going. To remedy this a little, the deep valley in Magdalen Road was filled and paved in 1599, and the dip in Holloway Street in 1605.

Many of these glimpses into the life of the city come from John Hooker (1523-1601), appointed Exeter's first chamberlain in 1555, who sorted out the accumulated archives, compiled a history of Exeter up to 1583, and in 1584 put into print the duties of the various officers. For instance, the porters

must, every night, shut and make fast, the City's Gates, at Ten of the Clock at Night in the Summer, and at Nine of the Clock in Winter; and must open the said Gates at Four of the Clock in the Morning in the Summer, and at Five of the Clock in the Winter. Also, if any Post happen to come ... Also, if any Hue-and-Cry shall happen to be ... Also, if any Tumults, Uproars, Escapes of Prisoners, Firing of Houses ... forthwith close and make fast the Gates.

48 Several other important buildings also had elaborately carved doors. This is no.10 in the Cathedral Close. The centre part would admit a person; the whole door would open for horses entering the yard.

The piped water-supply was to be kept clean and orderly by the Scavengers, who also had to see 'that no private Person do incroach the Common Commodity of the Waters therein for Brewing, Washing, or any such like use, other than for Dressing of their Meats, and such like'. In other words, the trickle of spring water from the conduit spouts was only for drinking and cooking. River-water was to be used for washing and cleaning.

Hooker loved Exeter and had trees planted in every available space in the city. Hooker's nephew Richard, 'Judicious Hooker', was born in Heavitree c.1553 and died in 1600. His statue has sat on the cathedral green since 1907. While a clerk at Corpus Christi he walked to and from Oxford each term for three years, until his patron, the Bishop of Salisbury, lent him a horse. He was ordained in 1581. He wrote a famous defence of the Church of England as established under Elizabeth I, *Of the lawes of ecclesiasticall politie*, promoting charity and tolerance towards Catholics and Calvinists.

Although its purpose was to supply a philosophical and logical basis for the Anglican church, it is also regarded as a landmark in English literature because of 'the stateliness and grace of its language'. It has been said to have 'more philosophical value than theological, and more literary value than either'.

One Sunday in 1581 a crowd was watching bear-baiting near Paris Street when the wooden stand collapsed. Seven were killed and many injured. On 7 August 1582 there was a happier entertainment. After the wedding in St Stephen's Church of the Earl of Bath and the daughter of the Earl of Bedford, Elizabeth, who had been born in Bedford House, the citizens presented them with a silver-gilt jug and basin, and laid on a grand cavalcade or 'triumph' in Southernhay.

Exeter paid towards the cost of supplying three ships when the Spanish Armada threatened the realm in 1588. Queen Elizabeth wrote to thank the 'ever-faithful' city. Exeter adopted the phrase as its motto: *Semper fidelis*.

Chapter 6

Serges and Sieges

By the early 17th century Exeter's woollen trade was steadily increasing in volume and value. Dyeing yellow, blue, green and black began to be practised on an industrial scale. Red dye was expensive and used more sparingly. Exeter specialised in light-weight serges, exporting them not just across the Channel and the North Sea but also to the lands of the eastern Mediterranean. The ships came home (if they escaped the dreaded Algerian pirates) laden with spices and wines, bringing large profits to the city's merchant venturers.

A school for their sons was started in 1633 which had roots going back 400 years, and which was to branch out to create four of Exeter's main educational establishments. The Long brothers had endowed a hospital just inside the east gate in *c.*1238, assigning to it family property bordering the nearby brook (which was therefore already known as the Longbrook). The hospital was a religious foundation, dedicated to St John the Baptist, housing five priests, six singing boys and twelve poor people. It was shut when the priories were dissolved, but the solid stone buildings and large church were subsequently used for dwelling-houses, a fleece market, a gunpowder store, a boys' workhouse and a grammar school. The church nave was divided into two floors; Latin and Greek were taught upstairs, and the Free English School occupied the ground floor. The latter supplied the pupils with uniform gowns and caps, leading to their nickname of Blue Boys. The buildings were modernised in 1859; in 1877 the name of the school was changed to St John's Hospital School, and the school survived until 1931. Hele's (now part of St Peter's) and Exeter School moved to new premises in 1840 and 1880 respectively, and both claim descent from the Grammar School. A Blue Maids' School was opened in Mary Arches Street in 1656, the forerunner of the Maynard.

49 St John's Hospital School before the 1859 rebuilding. The frontage onto the High Street was lost when the former priory church building was demolished to make way for a new Post Office building in 1880. One of the Blue Boy statues was placed in Princesshay in 1957 to mark the position of the entrance to the main school buildings.

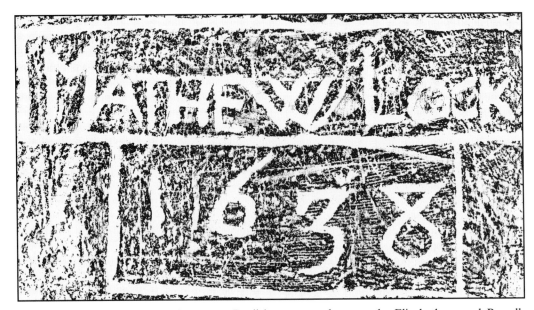

50 Matthew Locke, the most important English composer between the Elizabethans and Purcell, or, as Roger North put it, 'since Jenkins fell off', received his musical training in the cathedral choir and carved his name in the stonework of the organ loft in 1638. He later became court composer to Charles II and organist to his queen.

51 Bartholomew Yard by moonlight, looking northwards over the city walls. This peaceful scene records the midnight burial of the last cholera victim in August 1832, after which the cemetery was closed.

A lieutenant from Norwich came sight-seeing in 1634. He reported that the cathedral had 'a stately rich high Seat for the Bishop' and also 'a delicate, rich and lofty Organ which had more additions than any other, as fayre Pipes of an extraordinary length, and of the bignesse of a man's Thigh, which with their Vialls, and other sweet Instruments, the tunable Voyces, and the rare Organist [John Lugge], together, makes a melodious and heavenly Harmony... .' At this time the choir-master was Edward Gibbons (elder brother of Orlando) and Matthew Locke was a chorister. Locke's later career at court may have sprung from meeting the future King Charles II in 1644, when the prince lodged at the Deanery from 28 July until September, or perhaps their paths crossed later, when they both took refuge in the Netherlands.

By 1637 the cathedral yard had become the last resting-place of so many Exonians in the space of a thousand years that the rising ground level threatened to darken the cathedral windows. It was decided to close the yard to burials for 16 years. It was levelled and railed in, using 100 oaks from the city's stock in Duryard. A new cemetery was consecrated on 24 August 1637, St Bartholomew's Day, which gave the name Bartholomew to the street alongside it, previously known as Britayne.

During the Civil War Exeter was constantly under siege or attack from one party or the other. At the outset, a majority in the City Chamber supported Parliament. Exeter became the Puritans' HQ. It withstood assaults by Cornish royalist armies in November and December 1642. In the following spring the Earl of Bedford had the walls strengthened to carry cannon and to withstand artillery. Provisions were stockpiled. The areas outside the city gates were cleared of trees and houses. Defensive ditches were dug. The royalists captured key positions outside the walls and besieged the city from 19 June 1643. On 31 July, 1,000 defenders sallied out over Exebridge and drove the royalists out of the manor-house on Flowerpot field. (The cannonballs and shot fired that day can be seen in the museum.) But the rest of Devon was falling to Prince Maurice. The Duke of Bedford changed sides, and the Exeter garrison surrendered, marching out of the gates on 7 September. Sir John Berkeley took over as

52 The 'Tudor' house probably took its name from the local Tedder family. Prettily shaped slates originally covered the entire façade. Inside, a one-piece newel post rises through all four floors, and a musket-ball embedded in a beam of an upstairs room shows that the house stood through the sieges of the Civil War.

governor, and set up a mint to pay the troops. The following May the queen fled here from Oxford and was delivered of her ninth and last child in Bedford House on 16 June. Little Henrietta was christened in the cathedral on 21 July, by which time her mother had already gone home to France. Her father, busy fighting, saw the baby briefly on 26 July. The City Chamber gave the king £500. He could see that the city was prospering. He mentioned that his army could do with new shoes. Exeter gave him another £200 to buy 3,000 pairs. In September he was given a further £500. The city held out against Parliament for two and a half years, but agreed terms with Fairfax in

April 1647. The little princess was to be allowed to leave with her household and possessions. (In 1661 she would be married to the younger brother of Louis XIV, and by 1670 she was dead, possibly poisoned for acting as go-between for the French court and her fond eldest brother, Charles II.) The castle and its towers were to be demolished. The cathedral, churches and clergy were not to be harmed. This last undertaking proved worthless. The unruly Puritans ran into the cathedral to convert it into an ammunition store. They smashed the window glass, destroyed the books and struck the heads off the statues. They tore down the cathedral organ pipes and 'went up and down the streets, Piping with them, and meeting some of the Choristers ... scoffingly told them, "Boyes we have spoyled your trade, you must go and sing hot Pudding Pies"'. They also broke down the gates to the close, and turned elderly canons out of their houses, which were used for hospitals or slaughter-

houses or set on fire. The bishop's palace became the stable for their oxen and sheep. From 1657 to 1662 the cathedral was divided into East Peter's and West Peter's by a brick wall, for the separate worship of the congregationalist Independents and the Presbyterians. The Lady Chapel was converted into a library.

Only four of the city's 19 parish churches were to be retained for worship: St Mary Arches, St Edmund's, St Petrock's and St Mary Major. The others were to be sold. In many cases the parishioners bought them back. Allhallows on the Walls was an exception: it had taken a battering during the war and was left to deteriorate.

Royalists plotting to restore the monarchy used to meet at an inn just beyond the city's boundary-stone on the Bath Road. The swarthy complexion of Charles, the next king, had caused his mother to call him 'My black boy'. The inn-sign was a coded reference to

53 John Gendall's view of St Thomas from Exebridge shows the *Seven Stars* on the right. This inn had provided an upstairs room for George Fox to hold a Quaker meeting in 1657, and in 1728 John Gay's company performed *The Beggar's Opera* there.

54 In 1680 the wharfage reverted to the city chamber; they dredged the river, extended the stone quay, built a covered unloading bay and a brick Custom House where contraband tobacco was burned in the stove known as the 'King's Pipe'. The pool was enlarged: '100 sail of ship may safely ride therein'. The custom house originally had an open arcade.

this. Citizens rejoiced when his accession was proclaimed on 11 May 1660. A hogshead of good claret was fixed in each of the three public conduits. The siege trenches and dilapidations of the war were made good. Trinity Green was consecrated as an additional burial ground in 1664; the rest of Southernhay was levelled, and planted with 200 young elms. Another 200 were planted on Northernhay, to restore its charms as England's earliest pleasure-garden: it dated back to 1612. In 1672 the king gave the city a portrait of his Exeter-born sister, now dead.

The canal was extended to Topsham in 1676 and made deep enough for barges up to 16 tons. Ships off-loaded into seven lighters owned by the city. The Elizabethan quay was extended to make a waterfront twice as long, 483 ft. instead of 230 ft. A handsome Custom House was built in 1680, with cellars for storage and accommodation upstairs for the

excise officers, who were responsible for collecting dues on goods landed anywhere between the rivers Axe and Teign, not just the cargoes being unloaded below their windows. They had to chase local smugglers, who could be found leading pack-horses laden with tea or brandy up the narrow Devon lanes. The new Custom House was constructed of brick. It is the oldest surviving brick building in Exeter. Brickfields were beginning to make use of the local clay. The conical chimney kilns rose among the church steeples all around the city.

In 1680 James Duke of Monmouth toured the West Country to raise support for his cause. He came through Exeter with 500 horsemen and 900 young men in white uniform. After his defeat in 1685 Judge Jeffreys held one of his 'Bloody Assizes' in the Guildhall here, sending 80 rebels to the Heavitree gallows.

55 Blackboy Road looks towards the cathedral, St Sidwell's and leafy Rougemont, but in the foreground are the 100-feet-high cones of the brick-kilns built in 1834 to employ the inmates of the workhouse on Heavitree Road. Exeter gardeners know how suitable the clay is for making bricks.

56 The first St Paul's church may have been a Celtic foundation. This replacement of 1680 predated Queen Street and its market-hall, but was pulled down in 1930.

Jonathan Trelawney, Bishop of Bristol, was one of the seven bishops sent to the Tower for refusing to read out King James' 1687 Declaration of Indulgence. 20,000 Cornishmen began marching to London 'to know the reason why'. They had reached Exeter when they heard that all the bishops had been released, and the demonstrators went home.

On 5 November 1688 William of Orange landed at Brixham. His troops marched through mud and mist, needing a change of clothes when they reached Exeter. (Some needed nursing and were cared for in the Blue Maids' Hospital. The citizens sent in a bill to the king, and invoiced Queen Anne in 1706 to say that £345 4s. 2½d. was still outstanding.) On the following day, William came riding up Stepcote Hill with an impressive entourage which included '200 Blacks brought from the Plantations of the Netherlands in America, in Imbroyder'd Caps lined with white Fur ... 200 Finlanders in Bear skins taken from the Wild Beasts they had slain ... pages to support the prince's Banner, GOD AND THE PROTESTANT RELIGION ... and the Prince on a Milk White Palfrey, all in bright armour, and 42 Footmen running by him'. He did not think much of the state of the walls: 'I could take this city with baked apples'. He lodged at the Deanery waiting for assurances that it was safe to ride on to London. Bishop Trelawney was due to transfer to Exeter from the see of Bristol, but there was a delay. As King James crossed from Whitehall to Lambeth on his way to exile in France, he had thrown the Great Seal of England into the Thames, so the necessary documents could not be completed.

57 Stepcote Lane was the steep main road from the river crossing to the city centre until 1778, when a new bridge was aligned with Fore Street, and a linking viaduct was pushed through the city wall.

58 In 1694 a water engine was installed in the New Mill leat below Exe Street. The leat drove a wheel to pump water up through 18-inch wooden pipes to a reservoir behind the Guildhall (in use until 1833). Steam power was not needed. The huge cistern held 600 hogsheads of water, which was piped to houses in the city centre.

The following February when William and Mary were proclaimed King and Queen the conduits again ran with wine. Trade increased. Foreign merchants settled here to enjoy the new religious freedom. By 1700 the canal could carry ships over 100 tons. A sugar house and a glass house joined the paper-mills at Countess Wear, together employing hundreds.

Exeter was now at the height of its prosperity, the third largest city after London, with a population of about 13,000. Celia

Fiennes described the busy woollens industry in 1698:

> Carriers' wagons bring cloths from the loom ... They lay them to soack in vrine, then they soape them ... and put them into the fulling-mills and soe work them in the mills drye till they are thick enough ... then they turne water into them and so scower them ... they dry them in racks ... and huge large fields occupy'd this way almost all round the town which is to the river side ... they fold them with a paper between each fold.

A large proportion of the local population was kept busy shearing sheep, transporting fleeces, selling at market, carding, spinning, weaving in cottages, collecting urine, working the fulling-mills, dyeing, stretching the cloth on tenterhooks to dry in the rack-fields, raising a nap with teasels, trimming with shears, baling the finished cloth and loading it onto wagons and ships. Daniel Defoe, touring England in 1724-6, saw

> a city famous for two things, that 'tis full of gentry, and good company, and yet full of trade and manufacture also; the serge market, next to the market at Leeds, is the greatest in England; at this market is generally sold ... sometimes a hundred thousand pounds value in serges in a week.

Distinctive green baize aprons with red strings were worn 'by almost every other man you meet, all freemen of the Incorporated Company of Weavers, Fullers and Shearmen'. Even at the end of the century the members of this guild were known as the 'Golden Tuckers'—'from their habit of early clearing the market of their most expensive luxuries'.

Defoe was writing at a time when a weekly six-horse coach service had begun the run to Bath and Bristol, carrying six inside and taking three days. London was still six days distant, travelling non-stop.

Chapter 7

Georgian Exeter

A violent storm one night in November 1703 wrecked ships at sea, and in the city ripped the roofs off houses and blew chimney-stacks down. In the Cathedral Yard many of the elms that had stood there for nearly a century were torn up by the roots. The Dean and Chapter cleared away all the elms and made a fresh start with young lime trees, but these did not thrive and were replaced with elms again. Meanwhile, just as a growing tree is continually adding another outer ring, the living city itself was about to develop a surrounding zone of brick-built crescents, terraces, meeting-houses, prisons, barracks, theatres and a hospital, reflecting changes in society and in fashion.

John Baring, posthumous son of a Lutheran minister, came from Bremen in 1717 to learn the woollen trade. He lodged in Palace Gate and attended the dissenters' services in James' Meeting nearby. He studied well and married well, picking the daughter of a wealthy local grocer. By 1737 he could afford to move into Larkbeare; he filled the grounds with large press-shops, packing-rooms and rackfields. Robert Dymond wrote of these times that 'only three persons in Exeter possessed private carriages: Mr. Baring the wealthy cloth merchant, the Recorder and the Bishop'. There was only one wheeled conveyance for hire in the city then, otherwise it was horseback or sedan-chair—or one walked. (Municipal regulations governed the charges for sedan chairs. By 1805, 300 yards from Eastgate to the Bedford Theatre cost 6d., but 9d. after midnight.)

In 1748 Baring's three sons inherited the flourishing manufacturing and export business. Two of them founded a bank in 1768 which became the London merchant bank, Baring Bros. It has been claimed that the Baring family virtually ran the country during the reign of the four Georges, and helped to finance the British empire. In 1770 the eldest son returned to Exeter, bought the manor of Heavitree, a large area which included Mount Radford, the hill above Larkbeare, and built himself a mansion there. The middle son left £6,000,000 when he died in 1810. This was the kind of money to be made then from merchandise and merchant-banking.

The headmaster of Blundell's School in Tiverton, Samuel Wesley, died in 1739. His brothers John and Charles rode to Devon to comfort his widow, and John was invited to preach in Exeter. On the Sunday morning he spoke in Mary Arches on the text 'The kingdom of God is not meat and drink; but righteousness, and peace, and joy in the Holy Ghost'. The rector could not find anything undoctrinal in the sermon, but he asked Wesley not to preach in the afternoon: 'It is not guarded; it is dangerous. It may lead people into enthusiasm or despair'. Four years later, Charles Wesley preached in the open air in Exeter 'to about a thousand sinners, mostly gentlemen and ladies with some clergy'. Other dissenters had their meeeting-houses by now, but the new Wesleyan Methodists were mobbed and assaulted when they gathered for worship, and Catholics were celebrating mass only in the greatest secrecy, in an upper back room of *King John's Tavern* in South Street. The established church was less fervent: the satirist Andrew Brice describes 'sleepy maids sent to early service at the cathedral for the good of their lie-abed mistresses' souls'.

59 The Devon and Exeter Hospital in Southernhay was designed and erected by John Richards in 1742-3. It remains handsome and useful 250 years later, whereas its out-of-town replacement has had to be demolished after only 25 years. This photograph from *c*.1910 shows a St John ambulance near the main entrance.

In January 1741 the cathedral had elected a new dean, Dr. Alured Clarke. He had recently established a hospital in Winchester. At that time there were new hospitals in London, but none between Bristol and Land's End. Dr. Clarke was not well, but he vowed not to sleep until Exeter had a hospital. By 27 August a start had been made. The dean died nine months later, and the first patients were admitted in 1743.

Another innovation was the synagogue built in 1763 near Mary Arches Street. It is thought to be the second earliest in England.

The Duke of Bedford came to Exeter in 1769 to receive the freedom of the city. He had recently helped to negotiate a peace-treaty with France, and the local woollen traders feared competition from the French silk industry. An unfriendly crowd surrounded the Duke outside the castle; he could not make the short journey home but had to shelter in neighbouring Bampfylde House. He no longer felt welcome in Exeter. Shortly after, he allowed Bedford House to be demolished. A local builder, Robert Stribling, acquired the site in 1773 and designed a circus of houses. At first only 14 were completed, forming a crescent, not yet a circus. To achieve carriage-access, the city wall was broken through for 'an avenue across the Fosse of Southernhay'.

A certain 'Civis' wrote to the *Exeter Flying Post* in 1772 that the opening of the turnpike roads had brought 'families of Fortune and Distinction' to settle here. 'Many others would but not a House is to be obtained. A number of handsome houses will soon be erected on Southernhay.' Urban sprawl had begun. The citizens lost the use of Southernhay Green for recreation. The Lammas Fair and Horse Fair had to move. The grass would be 'surrounded with iron Palisadoes' to form private gardens.

50 The Barings and the Bowrings were among the wealthy Unitarians who built George's Meeting in South Street in 1760, naming it after the new king, George III. The carved pulpit was brought from their older meeting-house in James Street. The building was used for worship until 1987. Until then it remained a rare, perfect, unspoilt Georgian meeting-house.

51 Until the mid-18th century hardly any Devon roads were usable by wheeled traffic. Pack-horse trains used horse-ways three feet wide. Roads to market were eight feet wide. The Exeter Turnpike Trust of 1753 was the first in Devon. It built roads 30 feet wide. George Townsend drew the tollgates; this one is at Red Cow, below St David's Hill.

62 In 1603 the western pier of Exebridge needed a new cut water. Toisa's broken cross nearby was re-used in this practical way. When the medieval bridge was demolished in 1778, a merchant called William Nation purchased Toisa's cross and installed it at the corner of his High Street house (Bodley's birthplace) to protect it from the buffeting of sleds carrying bales of woollen goods from a Gandy Street store-room.

The city's streets had always catered for people on foot or horseback, or at most with a train of pack-animals. The alleys were too narrow for carriages or wagons. The Northgate was the first of the city's gates to be sacrificed to the convenience of wheeled traffic, in 1769. A year later, the Great Conduit was moved from the middle of the road so that carts could pass. In 1778 a new three-arched Exe-bridge was completed. Five further arches took the carriageway, New Bridge Street, across the leats of Exe Island to join lower Fore Street. It had taken three horses to pull a wagon up Stepcote Hill. The new approach to the city centre was only slightly less steep. Eastgate was taken down in 1784, and Westgate and Watergate in 1815.

The massive Southgate still served as the city's prison. Andrew Brice wrote:

Ten Men less room within this Cave,
Than five Mice in a Lantern have.

The common sewer from Southernhay ran under the felons' dungeon; debtors imprisoned upstairs were allowed to stand on the roof for fresh air. They used to let down an old shoe on a string to collect cash from passers-by. In 1779 John Howard said it was one of the most unwholesome and dismal places of confinement he had ever seen, but it was not demolished until 1819, when a new prison was ready on the opposite side of the city, where the *Rougemont Hotel* stands today. By then there was also a County Prison, facing it across the

Longbrook. On 19 June 1786 there was a balloon ascent from the Castle Yard, only three years after Montgolfier's exploit.

In 1789 George III, Queen Charlotte and two of their daughters stayed at the Deanery. Peter Pindar satirised the king's comments on the cathedral:

Neat, neat, clean, very clean,
Yes, very clean and neat;
D'ye mop it, mop it, Mr. Dean
Mop, mop it, every week?

By now, mail coaches could reach London from Exeter in 24 hours. The heavier carrier's wagon, drawn by eight shire horses, still took four and a half days. Every day except Sunday one team set out from Exeter, and one from St Paul's, and plodded steadily at two m.p.h. covering about 40 miles a day. The city's Post Office changed premises often during the next 100 years. At this time it occupied part of the cloisters adjacent to the cathedral's west front. The letters were delivered throughout the city by an old woman and her two daughters, carrying baskets. The post for London left promptly at noon. Anyone who had just missed it had to pay an extra twopence to an enterprising rider standing by, who would catch it up at Honiton.

Joanna Southcott was a domestic servant and upholstress in Exeter in 1792, when she claimed that God had chosen her (at the age of 42) to be the mother of Christ at his Second Coming. Twenty poor harvests between 1792 and 1814, leading to high prices and food riots, were taken as portents of the Last Days. Joanna moved to London and published 65 books and pamphlets before dying in 1814 without giving birth to a saviour, but she left a box to be opened in the presence of 24 bishops. Nobody is sure now which is the genuine box.

The Coade family, inventors of an artificial stone and proprietors of the London factory which supplied carved keystones and other decorations for most of England's Georgian terraces, also stemmed from Exeter. The city's brick-kilns were to remain busy, baking the soil on which they stood, for another 150 years, but their output was perhaps never used to such handsome effect as in the houses of Southernhay and Colleton Crescent, Barnfield Crescent and Bedford Circus.

63 Colleton Crescent was built on the cliff above the Quay in 1802-14, one of many terraces designed and built by the brothers Matthew and Thomas Nosworthy, mostly in brick, with round-headed doors ornamented with Coade keystones. The Nosworthys built the *New London Inn* (1790s), Barnfield Crescent (1792), most of Southernhay, and Dix's Field, where they chose to live themselves.

64 In the 1820s the Quaker banker Joseph Sparkes put up a stuccoed terrace of six handsome houses commanding an unparalleled view of the estuary. Called Pennsylvania after the settlement in the Americas, it has since given its name to the entire hillside suburb that has gradually crept up the surrounding slopes.

65 *Above left*. In 1849 Dr. Thomas Shapter published an account of Exeter's cholera epidemic, illustrated with woodcuts by his friend John Gendall which recorded not only the special circumstances of 1832-3 but also many street scenes which had been altered since then. River water was sold by the bucket, three for a penny, from water-carts, or water-bearers with hooped yokes.

66 *Above right*. In 1750 a 'New Cut' was made through the city wall near the cathedral. In 1814 mayor Burnet Patch had a little iron bridge built over it to facilitate the Muraltie Walk, the perambulation of the walls which followed the mayor-choosing.

67 Longbrook Valley is pictured in 1831, between the elms of Northernhay and the prison (rebuilt 1810), with the 'pepperpot' St David's (1816) in the distance. Cossins reminisced: 'Before the North road was cut there was a succession of fields from Barrack Road to St David's Church, a very pleasant walk and a resort for children gathering buttercups and daisies'.

68 While building Barnfield Crescent the labourers uncovered a strong spring supplying an angular bath of grey bricks, very hard burnt, strongly cemented, with steps leading down to it. This discovery inspired the erection of the Public Hot and Cold Baths in Southernhay, making use of the abundant water. It stood above Chichester Place.

69 Exeter from Pennsylvania Hill, after G.B. Campion, published 1832. About 70 passenger coaches left Exeter daily in the 1830s. Pennsylvania Road had just been cut through for wheeled traffic, providing a route that was less precipitous than the turnpike road over Stoke Hill.

70 Built in 1768, this establishment was the first in England to be called an *hôtel* when its French owner
advertised in September 1770. It has been called the *Royal Clarence Hotel* since the Duchess of Clarence, wife
of the future William IV, slept here in July 1827. It could accommodate balls, assemblies and concerts. Franz
Liszt performed here in August 1840.

71 In 1817-24 Caleb Hedgeland made a wooden scale model (10 ft. by 6 ft.) showing the city's streets and buildings before the many changes that had recently been made. The Treasurer's house stood against the cathedral's north tower until 1798. St Michael's Gate can be seen at Broadgate (removed 1819). Behind old St Mary Major the post office stands alongside the cathedral's west front.

Chapter 8

The early 19th century

Mayor Thomas Floud determined to start the new century well. He brought in a by-law in 1800: citizens were to sweep the pavement in front of their houses three times a week. While he was about it, he solved the parking problem too, by 'suppressing the practice of leaving horses, carts &c. in the streets'. He was commended for 'changing the appearance of the public streets from the most disgusting filth to perfect cleanliness'. Soon after, the city paved the footways with Moor Stones (granite) and the carriageways with Pebble Stone (cobbles). It was proposed that 'the names of each street and lane should be painted at their several corners'. Some parishes carried this out and some did not.

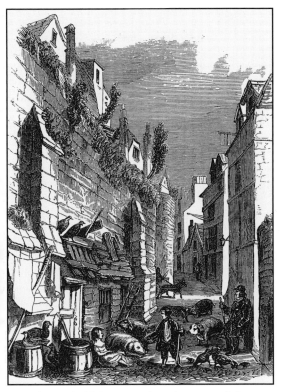 

72 Pigs and chicken were kept in most of the courts between the cottages. This is Rack Close Lane, typical of the west quarter. In the lower part of the city, houses were built on and against the town walls.

73 Here houses of the Elizabethan period at Cricklepit abut the town wall. There is a fulling-mill to the left. The mill-leat is being used for laundering.

Exeter was the first place in Devon to install gas lighting in the main street. The gasworks opened in 1817, one of the first in a provincial city.

The Napoleonic wars had disrupted overseas trade. When it resumed, Exeter was outstripped by the northern manufacturing towns. The city still had busy mills, bonded warehouses for imported wine, factories, tanneries, markets and iron foundries, but it had also become a fashionable address for the families of naval and military men, somewhere for the retirement of wealthy merchants, bankers and successful officers of the East India Company. Flora Macdonald's son was one of the latter, settling into a little house on the Old Tiverton Road. Richard Ford, author and traveller, boasted to his friends that Exeter was 'quite a capital, abounding in all that London has, except for its fog and smoke'.

A theatre had been incorporated into Bedford Circus in 1787. The Kembles played here, and even Sarah Siddons herself. From 1796 the theatre put on annual benefits for the hospital. Edmund Kean, the uncontrolled but brilliant tragedian, appeared here in December 1811 and was well received, then walked to Bath in January but was not engaged for the theatre there. In 1813 he appeared 40 times in Exeter before taking his young family on foot to Dorchester, where his older little son died, perhaps from the hard travelling life. However, the manager of Drury Lane saw Kean on stage there and gave him a three-year contract. Coleridge wrote of Kean: 'To see him was like reading Shakespeare by flashes of lightning'.

A more restful treat, on Sunday evenings, was to walk across the Longbrook fields to the cavalry barracks next to the County Prison to listen to the regimental bands. The prisoners probably enjoyed it too, in their cells. The Devon and Exeter Institution had been founded in 1813, and provided a learned library and stimulating meeting-place. Subscription Rooms were opened in 1820 in London Inn Square.

Barton Place, two miles north of the city, is believed to have been the model for Barton Park in Jane Austen's *Sense and Sensibility*. For such fashionable households, nurserymen such as Veitch, father of the Chelsea Flower Show, were importing exotic stock. Luccombe

had developed the famous fast-growing evergreen Exeter oak; specimens were planted in Southernhay and many local pleasure-grounds as well as on gentlemen's estates. Prince Albert bought some for the avenue at Osborne.

John Bowring, born in Great Larkbeare in 1792, was preparing for a great future, learning dozens of foreign languages at the quay, where there were ships 'from all nations', and spending Sundays dreaming during the sermons in George's Meeting. He became a traveller, economist, adviser to Jeremy Bentham and governor of Hong Kong, and introduced the florin as a first step towards a British decimal coinage.

Cycling in Exeter began surprisingly early. On 3 April 1819 a celeripede was exhibited in the playground of the Exeter Grammar School. On the 24th of the same month a three-wheeler was ridden from the turnpike gate at Marypole Head (the junction of Pennsylvania Road and Rosebarn Lane) to the bottom of Longbrook Street, a four-minute mile on a bumpy road.

There were balls and parties at the time of the assizes. Cossins reports: 'The March Assizes were always the largest, as many more robberies were committed in the winter nights than in the summer'. Anthony Trollope and his brother Thomas often visited Exeter in their boyhood in the 1820s, travelling on the 'Devonport Mail'. 'At the time it was possibly the fastest in England, "the Quicksilver Mail", travelling at full gallop at about 12 m.p.h.', armed with pistols and blunderbuss against highwaymen. At inn-stops the horses were changed in less than a minute. The Trollope boys enjoyed excursions to Marypole Head or strawberry and cream parties at Hoopern Bowers, 'always with a bevy of pretty girls'.

The fun stopped when Exeter was badly hit by cholera in 1832 and 1833. A local doctor, Thomas Shapter, wrote a detailed account of the epidemic: the worst affected areas, sanitary measures, the emergency burial grounds (in Berry Meadow and near Rowe's Barn Lane). His book was already at the printers in 1849 when his artist friend, John Gendall, offered him several illustrations, which Shapter welcomed, realising that they recorded not only the melancholy events at the time of the epidemic, but also 'places and customs which have since passed away: the progress of the last 17 years in destroying "Old Exeter" is

74 Cholera raged through the poorer quarters in 1832, sometimes taking whole families in the space of a few hours. Here a coffin is being carried along Goldsmith Street, past St Paul's church.

75 Every effort was made to combat infection. Here Butchers' Row is being fumigated.

76 Bedding and clothing was incinerated at Lion's Holt and on the river bank, near the drying racks of the cloth industry.

77 The streets and gutters were washed down. The fire plugs were opened to build up a good puddle, then men threw the water over the cobbles with wooden shovels.

remarkable'. Many of the changes were attempts to improve public hygiene. The Longbrook was culverted at the lowest point of Longbrook Street, where it had previously formed a picturesque willow-hung pool crossed by a footbridge. The Chutebrook was culverted for most of its length. Drinking water came from new works drawing from the river a mile north of the quayside. Market stalls were cleared from the crowded streets into two purpose-built halls. The cattle market was moved from Bartholomew Street to the Bonhay. The narrowest alley in the city was named Parliament Street as an expression of disdain for the 1832 Reform Bill. In contrast, a broad and handsome thoroughfare was created to lead north from High Street, and named Queen Street. At first it terminated at Northernhay. Beyond were fields, gardens and orchards on each side of the Longbrook valley. But when the Turnpike Trust cut the New North Road in 1833, along the farther bank, linking Cowley Road and London Inn Square, it was suggested that Queen Street could be

extended over a viaduct to meet it. This was done in 1835-40.

Families who could afford it moved from the crowded city-centre to the healthy heights of the surrounding green slopes. St Leonard's was popular, being fairly level once one had coped with Bull Hill and the Chutebrook valley. Messrs Hooper the developers bought the Mount Radford estate from Sir Thomas Baring in 1825 and erected pretty stucco villas along Wonford Road and St Leonard's Road. In 1833 they improved access by building a level viaduct across Bull Meadow. Carriage-horses had a much easier time now, thanks to this improvement, and the Iron Bridge and Queen Street. Carthorses still had to strain to ascend Holloway Street, Fore Street and North Street.

Notable society events of these years included the christening in St Sidwell's of little Sabine Baring Gould, who had been born in 1 Dix's Field, Southernhay, on 28 January 1834. He grew up to become parson, squire, antiquarian, folklorist, father of a large family

78 Before the Queen Street viaduct bridged the Longbrook valley, horse-drawn carts and carriages from the north had no choice but the steep climbs and descents over St David's Hill. This view by P.V. Pitman also shows the older road, and the weather-vane marking the site of Northgate.

79 When the improvement commissioners were considering a bridge, an iron-founder called Russell from Blaina in Monmouthshire was in town selling iron lamp-posts and won the contract to design and supply the cast-iron arches. They came by sea in 1835.

80 The Queen Street façade of the Higher Market, shown here in an etching by P.V. Pitman, was designed by George Dymond, finished by Charles Fowler (famous as the architect of Covent Garden Market) and opened in 1838. It was saved from demolition in the 1960s and incorporated into a new shopping centre.

81 The main hall of the Higher Market, where local farmers and fishmongers rented trestle tables.

and author of many historical novels, but is perhaps best remembered for his hymns, which include 'Onward Christian Soldiers'. It was in 1834 too that Richard Ford settled in Heavitree, where he rebuilt an old house in Gothic style, and laid out 12 acres with Moorish terraces, patterned flower-beds, pines and cypresses. He wrote his *Hand-Book for Travellers in Spain* in a 'den' in the garden. This was not only an early example of the travel-book genre, but also a work of high literary quality, full of anecdotes and local colour as well as practical information. John Gendall painted Ford on the terrace with his wife, child, nanny and pet macaw.

In 1835 Charles Dickens was sent to Exeter to report on the hustings for the *Morning Chronicle*. The Eatanswill elections and the Fat Boy are the fictional fruit. In the same year an entrepreneur constructed vast catacombs in the hillside under Bartholomew Yard, for fashionable interments, but it proved too expensive, and attracted hardly any customers. Samuel Sebastian Wesley (grandson of Charles Wesley), the finest composer of church music of his time, was organist and Master of Music at the cathedral from 1835 to 1841. His nine-week-old daughter is buried in the Lower Cemetery alongside the catacombs, and when he himself died in Gloucester in 1876 he chose to be laid beside her. Franz Liszt toured England in 1840 with a small group, playing his own piano compositions interspersed with songs and duets. They performed in the *Royal Clarence Hotel*, which overlooked the grass and large trees in the Close, and Liszt wrote to his mistress that English cathedrals are more impressive than those in France because they are not crowded round with shops and other buildings.

Joseph Sparkes the Quaker banker had a seizure in July 1836 at his brother's house in Exeter, and, desiring to die in his own house he had himself carried in a sedan-chair up the long steep road to enjoy the panoramic views from the windows of no.1 Pennsylvania. He watched an early steamboat on the river. Times were changing. Exeter quay was now at its busiest. The canal basin was enlarged in 1830 Two massive warehouses, five storeys high were built on the quay in 1834-5, one by Messrs. Hooper, the other by Robert Cornish Sailing ships filled every berth. Horse-drawn sleds or 'truckamucks' pulled casks over the cobbles. 19th-century imports included Danubian corn, Swedish timber, French loaf sugar and North of England coal. Exports included barytes (mined at Christow and ground at the Quay mills). When Henry Phillpotts was chosen to be Bishop of Exeter in 1830 he decided to hire a small collier to carry from the deanery at Chester his wine his furniture and 60-70 tons of coal that he did not wish to leave behind.

When the railways came to Exeter the quay lost its rôle as chief dispatching centre for the cheap transport of goods and passengers.

Chapter 9

Trains, Trams, Tracts, Tennis

In 1808 James Kemp had written *Northernhay*, a poem addressed to Solitude, where the evening silence was broken only by the curfew's solemn sound, the screech-owl and the distant river. Later in the century 'Musopolus' [servant of the Muses] also sang of the evening, the curfew and the cawing of rooks, but now:

... from out the valley broke
Snowy whirls of shrieking smoke!
'Tis the form and 'tis the scream
Of the great familiar, Steam.

The Bristol and Exeter Railway reached St David's in 1844, and the London and South Western line was to disturb the peace of Northernhay from 1860. At midday on 1 May 1844 the first passenger train from Paddington arrived at the station at Red Cow, called St David's for greater dignity. Sir Thomas Acland travelled back on it that evening, and went to the Houses of Parliament at 10 p.m. to announce that he had still been in Exeter at 5.20 p.m. As Exeter time was still local time, the journey had been even shorter than it sounded, by 14 minutes. Railway timetables eventually brought about standard time-keeping, but it was not until 1880 that Greenwich Mean Time was enforced throughout the kingdom. However, the dean was persuaded to put the cathedral clock forward 14 minutes as early as 2 November 1852. A clock in Fore Street added an extra minute hand, so that it could show both railway time and Exeter time. This clock was called 'the moon of Fore Street', as its illuminated dial projected from the tower of St John's church high above the steep road. The Clock Tower in the New North Road (now a major landmark) was not built until 1897, replacing a simple obelisk and horse-trough. It commemorated the Queen's jubilee, at the head of Queen Street, named at the time of her coronation 60 years before.

The Great Western Railway leased the Bristol-Exeter line for five years, then took it over. Their chief engineer, Isambard Kingdom Brunel, approved the adoption of a new system for the next undertaking, the South Devon Railway extension to Plymouth: the Atmospheric System patented by Samuda

82 'A General View of the Pump and Passenger Stations at Exeter.' The Italian-style pumping station is on the left, and the simpler barn-like structure of St David's Station on the right.

Brothers and Clegg. It moved trains by suction, like the cash capsules in a bank. Pumping stations three miles apart created a vacuum in a pipe lying between the lines. The train inserted a piston in a slit in the pipe and flew along at up to 68 m.p.h. without any of the noise, soot or judder of a steam locomotive. A pump-house was built next to the station at Red Cow, and another by the estuary at Star Cross. The three roads just west of Exebridge would have needed so many level crossings that a 62-arch viaduct was built instead. By early 1845 a number of humble cottagers who had been in the way of this grand project had been ruthlessly unhoused.

The first trains to Teignmouth on this line were pulled by locomotives after all, but the atmospheric system was used for 12 months from September 1847. It was then abandoned because either rats or the salty sea air had damaged the leather flaps which maintained the vacuum.

By 1851 visitors could travel by train from Plymouth to London for the Great Exhibition. The Vivian family, travelling up from Cornwall, made a game of it from Plymouth as far as Exeter, wagering that Papa would go faster across Dartmoor in his carriage than Mama and the children on the South Devon Railway. It was a tie. Queen Victoria praised an unusual exhibit in the Crystal Palace, a model of the west front of Exeter Cathedral, nine feet high, made by Mrs. Kingdon from the pith of rushes from the canal, using only a gum-pot and a pair of scissors. Mrs. Kingdon had been born a Bodley and married into another well-known Exeter family. Among the visitors to the Exhibition was her six-year-old grandson, William Kingdon Clifford, of Longbrook Street, whose father was a High Street bookseller. William attended Dr. Templeton's Academy in Bedford Circus. At his aunt's house in London he was looking worried at bedtime. He did not think she could help him, but uncle might. He had been trying to calculate how many times the width of his penknife blade would go into the rim of their carriage-wheel. Uncle was able to reassure him that he had got it right. William was to become Second Wrangler at Cambridge, professor of

83 Two men out rabbiting in 1848 on the slopes above Exwick chapel (of 1842) look across to the city on its cliffs. St David's Station lies below them, but to the right, echoing the tower of Allhallows, is the campanile-like chimney of the pump-house of the atmospheric railway.

84 Two steam locos speeding towards the passengers waiting at the Exeter railway station in 1850, seen from Cowley Bridge Road.

85 This view of the rear of the hospital in Southernhay was drawn in 1852 by John Harris, a former surgeon, showing where the railway was not built, but where Western Way would later overrun the chestnut trees. The sketch also predates the Victorian extensions to the hospital, and the rebuilding of Wynards and of the Friends' meeting-house.

86 St Luke's teacher-training college, founded in 1840, was one of the earliest in England. New premises on the Heavitree Road were opened in 1855, two years after Besley had published this print. The tramp in the foreground is waiting for the nearby workhouse to open for the night.

applied mathematics at University College London, and an acclaimed teacher and free-thinker. His career was cut short by TB before he was 34. He had anticipated Einstein by suggesting that physical space is curved, and his 'geometric algebra' is now widely used in mathematics, physics and engineering. He also propounded a comprehensive philosophy, based on Darwin's theory of evolution. George Bernard Shaw wrote to his widow Lucy: 'You were lucky enough to be married to a clever man—cleverer than anyone except Einstein—even cleverer than ME!'

The middle of the century saw rioting on the streets and in the churches. Severe winters led to food-riots and protests at the price of bread. The mayor called out the dragoons from the cavalry barracks to protect the Guildhall from the angry mob. There were also violent clashes, with mud-throwing and rotten eggs, about the use of the surplice when preaching, thought to be a high-church practice. Bishop Phillpotts (1830-69) did not oppose the Tractarian movement, but changed his mind often enough on the Catholic question for some to regard him as a traitor, to the extent that Sidney Smith could write that he was

'living proof of the apostolic succession, in his case from Judas Iscariot'.

Tractarian ideals were embodied in a new church built on Mount Dinham in 1865-8 and described in a newspaper report as 'the finest church in Exeter next to the cathedral'. The inspiration came from Augustus Pugin, who had written that pointed arches and soaring lines were a truer representation of Christian belief than designs modelled on pagan Greek temples. The finance came from a man with local connections, William Gibbs, who had a family fortune based on the import of guano for fertiliser. He had provided most of the cost of Keble College Chapel at Oxford. He commissioned the architect Rhode Hawkins to design a chapel of ease for the almshouses and the Blind School in this part of St David's parish. The site already lay high above the Longbrook valley, and the new church of St Michael and All Angels was given a spire 220 ft. high, reputedly the fourth tallest in the kingdom.

Several events in Victoria's reign inspired elaborate street decorations. The Royal Agricultural Society met in Exeter in 1850. A baron of beef was roasted on gas jets in the castle yard, then carried shoulder-high along a leafy Queen Street to a marquee below Northernhay. For the Bath and West Show in June 1889 a replica of the Eastgate was constructed, as well as 12 evergreen arches over the main roads, each carrying an improving motto, such as 'He that would thrive must rise at five. He that hath thriven may lay till seven'.

Exeter Central is such a familiar sight below Northernhay that it is hard to believe that the plan in 1836 was to run the railway along the Chutebrook valley to the Quay, with the main station in the Barnfield. However, the Longbrook valley was used instead, the London and South Western Railway reached Queen Street in 1860, and on 19 July at 3 p.m., during a violent cloudburst, the first passenger train from Waterloo brought the railway's directors to a celebration dinner in a leaky marquee. On 1 February 1862 the Queen Street Station was linked to St David's via a tunnel under St David's Hill. The gradient is 1 in 37; there is no steeper slope between Exeter and London. The *Rougemont Hotel* was built opposite Queen Street station in 1876 to cater for rail passengers, at a cost of £30,000.

The death in 1861 of the Prince Consort, who had done so much for science and the arts, inspired fund-raising for a museum to be founded in his honour, which was to incorporate a Free Library, Reading Room, science classes and a School of Art. In 1868 J.B. Goodrich celebrated its opening:

> Here's the Museum of fair design,
> Carved and polished superbly fine ...
> Inwardly all is nicely plann'd,
> Corridors branching on either hand ...
> Students of Art and Literature
> Will draw, and read, and look demure,
> While others will information gain,
> Or just 'pop in' to dodge the rain.

A young sculptor, Harry Hems, had come to Exeter in 1866 to carve the decorations for this museum. He had trained as a cutler but had saved enough sixpences as an apprentice to cross the Channel, and had then gone on foot to Florence to learn sculpture. As he walked up St David's Hill, he picked up a lucky horseshoe and swore that one day he would fix it on the front of one of the best buildings in Exeter. He built up a large business, and eventually commissioned R. Medley Fulford to design the workshops which still stand in Longbrook Street, with the original horseshoe on the front. Hems moved into the adjacent house, which had been the childhood home of William Kingdon Clifford. Ecclesiastical and municipal carvings were dispatched by rail from Longbrook Street to grace cathedrals and parliament buildings in many countries. Hems was a tough employer but a generous benefactor, giving lavish Christmas dinners to the local 'old codgers'.

Tennis was a popular local sport. A club, called Victoria Park after its premises in St Leonard's, was founded in 1879. This makes it the second oldest tennis club in Britain, Queen's being older but Wimbledon and even the Lawn Tennis Association younger.

Henry Arthur Jones was a commercial traveller and self-taught playwright. He married in 1875 and rented The Hermitage at Exwick for the next six years. In December 1878 the Shakespeare season at the Theatre Royal was proving a disaster, and Jones was allowed to put on his own play 'It's Only Around the Corner'. Soon afterwards he gave up 'bagmanship' and devoted his life to 'the reform of the English Drama', writing dozens of moralistic plays. His friend George Bernard Shaw wrote to him in 1898: 'The missus thinks you vastly inferior to me as a dramatist (Shakespeare also); but she appreciates you as a man'. He had great ideals. Oscar Wilde laid down three rules for writing plays: 'The first rule is not to write like Henry Arthur Jones, the second and third rules are the same'. Nevertheless, Jones made a fortune.

On 5 September 1887 there was a terrible fire at the Theatre Royal when scenery caught alight and 160 members of the audience were unable to escape. Burning beams fell on the horses waiting at the cabstand. One bolted all the way to Marypole Head. The theatre was rebuilt and was the first in the country to install a fireproof curtain. The incident also led to national legislation requiring outward-opening exits in all places of entertainment. From 1889 until 1950 the new Theatre Royal put on a Christmas pantomime every year, the only theatre in the world with an uninterrupted record of 61 consecutive pantomimes.

87 In the winter months of 1857-8 the navvies levelling the bed for the London and South Western Railway cut off the cathedral's water supply, which had been piped from an ancient well at Lion's Holt for over 600 years. With pick and wheelbarrow they dug through the clay and into the underlying red sandstone.

88 The cathedral was left without water for nearly three years. The brickwork of the well had been renewed in 1836, but this was the first time that it had been completely investigated.

89 On 10 February 1858 the standpipe was found to rise through a lead disc 10 feet across, resting on channelled stone slabs. Lying on the bedrock and under the stones was a shiny copper coin of Nero (Roman emperor A.D. 54-68, i.e. when the legionary bath-house was being built).

90 Southernhay Gardens were railed in for the private use of residents, but here a crowd has gathered in the highest section near the fountain, possibly to greet men of the Queen's Ninth Royal Lancers, who returned to their Exeter depot in 1859 after capturing Delhi and putting down the mutiny in India.

91 The same early photographer pointed his apparatus northwards from his back room, over the roofs of the *Bude Hotel* at the top of Paris Street, past the spire of St Sidwell's church, to distant Pennsylvania.

92 The museum's Queen Street façade, in early French Gothic style, uses a variety of different coloured local stones. The architect, John Hayward, also designed several other important Exeter buildings, including St Luke's College and the Devon County Prison.

93 By 1870, Townsend's etching of 1848 (illustration 83) had been updated to emphasise Mount Dinham cliff and to include the new spires of St Michael's and St Mary Major, but above all to add the large train-shed of St David's Station and the track climbing steeply through a tunnel to Queen Street.

94 Queen Street Station before the First World War, viewed from almost the same spot as illustration 67. The London and South Western Railway had reached Exeter in 1860. Access was from the path below Northernhay Gardens, or down the adjacent slope. The station buildings were wooden, with roofs of different length sheltering the up and down platform and track.

95 St David's Station was rebuilt in 1912-4. This view from the water-tower shows the decorative urns on Fox's façade of 1862-4, the G.W.R. building inside it, the overall train-shed being dismantled and new platform canopies being built. Streatham Hall stands on the hill among its woods.

96 The Arcade, built in 1882, was an elegant shopping precinct sheltered from the traffic and the weather that ran from Eastgate to Southernhay. A grand officer would usher out the public at 6 p.m., pull on white gloves and make a ceremony of lowering the iron gates.

97 From 1837 to 1887 two front rooms in the Guildhall served as the police station. Excavation for new premises in Waterbeer Street, just behind the Guildhall, uncovered part of a Roman mosaic pavement. This was incorporated into the new entrance. When the shopping area was redeveloped in the 1960s, the whole floor was misidentified as Victorian and thrown away.

98 Horse-trams ran from the *Bude Hotel* to Heavitree from 1882, and from St David's station to the top of Blackboy Road from 1883, but the High Street tradesmen would not let them run through the city centre. The High Street is free from trams but open to carts and carriages. This view looks across London Inn Square to Sidwell Street. The G.P.O. of 1885 is on the right. The shop canopies are supported on poles which fit into slots in the kerb-stones.

99 Looking in the same direction as the previous photograph, but now there are tram-lines. By 1903 High Street traders had heard that Sidwell Street businesses were benefiting from the horse-drawn trams passing their doors, and they lifted their ban.

100 Looking in the opposite direction, westwards from London Inn Square. The entrance to the arcade can be seen set back on the left.

101 The Guildhall end of the High Street. Horses still outnumber motors by two to one. When the last horse-drawn tram gave way to the first electric tram on 4 April 1905 the Guildhall was the setting for the ceremony.

102 A tram passes the Cabbies' Rest at the 'Fountain' at the top of Sidwell Street. The drivers of the hansom cabs in the rank here could shelter from the rain and cold without being tempted to wait in a pub. The Earl of Shaftesbury had set up a Cabmen's Shelter Fund in 1889 to prevent drunken driving.

Cycling had become so popular by the end of the century that several clubs had been formed: the Exeter Rovers, the YMCA, the Exeter Cycling Club and so forth. In October 1890 there was a Cyclists' Carnival in aid of the Devon and Exeter Hospital. Clubs were invited from neighbouring towns. Two hundred cyclists came from Topsham alone. The procession included fire brigades, the Devon Volunteers Artillery Band and hand-bell ringers. The cyclists were in fancy dress: 'courtiers, clergymen, clowns, princes, costermongers, smugglers, country bumpkins and mashers'. No women took part. One cycle had fairy-lamps along its handles. A tricycle carried 17 large lanterns. One safety machine had 12 lanterns over the rider's head, surmounted by a Japanese parasol. At a rocket signal at 8 p.m. the bands began to play, and the cycles moved off from Bury Meadow along Queen Street, High Street and Sidwell Street until they reached the fountain, then back through the city to St Thomas, where they turned, across Commercial Road to South Street, along Southernhay, finally ending up in Bury Meadow again. £96 18s. 3½d. was collected.

The Albert Memorial College and the Devon and Exeter Hospital both added 'Royal' to their name on 19 July 1899 when the future George V and Queen Mary opened new wings for each.

In 1904 a new power station was needed for the electric tram system. It was built next to the Basin, convenient for the delivery of coal by barge. So much power was needed to carry a laden tram up Fore Street that only one at a time was supposed to attempt it. P.G. Martin, when a small boy, was on a tram when this rule was broken, a fuse blew, and they saw the tram ahead beginning to slip backwards. They got off.

In 1899 the Exeter Brick and Tile Company set up a factory on the Polsloe Priory Estate with machinery which could turn out 100,000 bricks every week. The band of red clay which runs through Pinhoe to Pennsylvania is particularly suited for brickmaking. It has also been used on many local cricket pitches to make a firm dry underlay for the turf.

103 From the gas-works: a sailing-barge near the canal's swing-bridges; the *Port Royal* on the river bank, on safer ground, the judges' lodgings (Larkbeare House), St Leonard's church (1876-84), St Leonard's Avenue and Weirfield Road (1890s) and the palatial Royal West of England School for the Deaf (1895-7) with its new wing of 1900.

104 A new Exebridge was opened on 29 March 1905. St Thomas was incorporated into the Exeter municipal area in 1899. Willey's iron-works and the new electricity works at the basin brought rush-hour numbers up to 3,000, and 10,000 crossed on Saturday evenings.

105 The new single-span steel bridge opened in 1905 was designed to accommodate the new electric trams. Here the tram proudly displays the name of its new destination.

106 The tramlines and overhead electric wires of the new system dominate the High Street, but there is still room for a bicycle and a horse-drawn cart.

107 Nursery gardens have surrounded the city for many centuries, supplying flowers, fruit and vegetables. The Sclater family grew tulips and daffodils in the orchards round Bowhill, and stored apples and ripening peaches in the spacious upstairs rooms of the house.

108 Harvesting sweet-scented Mrs. Simkin's pinks on the hillside below Hambeer Lane.

109 General Redvers Buller attended the unveiling on 9 September 1905 of the 13-feet-high bronze equestrian statue depicting himself in army greatcoat and plumed helmet. His record in South Africa was controversial, but crowds of local supporters were swollen by excursion train-loads from London and Bristol. He died on 2 June 1908, and the statue was draped funereally.

Chapter 10

20th-Century Exeter

Exeter City football team turned professional in 1908, joining the Southern league and adopting 'the Grecians' as their nickname. This name is rooted deeply in Exeter's history, and so is the past life of St James' football field. The youngest daughter of the 2nd Earl of Bedford was born in Bedford House and christened Margaret in St Stephen's church in July 1566. Nearly a century later, in December 1654, a charity was set up in her memory by her daughter, Lady Anne Clifford. The proceeds from renting out a field near St Anne's Chapel, called Mountstephen, were to pay 'yearly to the world's end' for the apprenticeship of 'one poor Child, Boy or Girl, born and residing in the parish of St Stephen'. The field was rented out for fattening pigs. Travelling menageries camped there each year. The old boys of St Sidwell School used it for football. Their team took the name of Exeter City in 1904 and took over the field for football only. The lease stipulated 'no menageries, shows, circuses or steam roundabouts'. In 1908 the supporters voted for the nickname 'the Grecians'. This was the traditional name for the inhabitants of St Sidwell's, which for centuries had been part of the city but outside the walls. Boys of the parish fought the city boys regularly during the annual ceremony of beating the bounds. The city boys wore blue uniforms, and carried blue Tory favours, and the St Sidwell boys wore yellow for the Whigs, and perhaps represented the ancient Greeks who had besieged Troy, since like them they were outside the city. Andrew Brice's epic on the elections of 1737 describes fights between the two mobs, the Blues and the Greeks, and he explains in a footnote that the Greeks are 'the rugged inhabitants of St Sidwell's' who contend with the city at football, while the townsmen are like the Trojans defending their ground. The local boys certainly knew the Homeric story of the Trojan war from their schoolbooks, just as their medieval predecessors (including Joseph of Exeter in the 13th century) had known it from medieval romances. In 1346 Robert Noble was mayor and had a beautiful daughter. One of her admirers composed this verse:

> As noble Helen was the cause
> Of ten years' war in Troy,
> So Helen Noble is the cause
> Of this my great annoy.

In July 1726 *The Siege of Troy* was enacted during the fair on Southernhay by puppets, with a large wooden horse, Troy in flames, and the 'Grecian' fleet sailing home across the sea. In 19th-century court cases plaintiffs from St Sidwell's were referred to as Greeks, and people writing to the local paper signed themselves Grecians. So the name was adopted, and a Grecian Gate was put up at the ground, and supporters flocked to games on foot or via the nearby railway halt.

Poverty in the West Quarter was alleviated by a soup kitchen in the Lower Market, hot dinners from the Exe Island Mission, and the Farthing Breakfast scheme. For the latter, citizens put aside the odd farthings they received at a time when most prices ended in elevenpence threefarthings, and handed them in at the *Express and Echo* office in High Street. A list of donors and amounts would be printed. Rich children would look eagerly to see their name in the paper. Poor children would pay a farthing for the subsidised breakfast: 'as much cocoa as you could drink, plus three door-steps of bread, one spread with butter and the other two with jam'.

Heavitree was not such a poor, crowded area. Exeter families went to stay there for healthy summer holidays: after all, it was a good mile away. As a settlement, standing at the crossing of ancient ridgeways, it may be older than Exeter. Its church was the mother church of the three early churches outside Exeter's walls: St Sidwell's, St David's and St Leonard's. Perhaps it was a feeling of superiority which made Heavitree resist annexation by Exeter in 1900 when St Thomas joined the city. It held out for 13 years, then on 24 November 1913 'Sergeant Snell at the stroke of midnight led a posse of police to take over the new area'. This added a population of 11,000 to Exeter's 49,000. Three existing wards (Heavitree, Polsloe and Wonford) were joined by three new creations: St Loyes', St Mark's and Whipton.

Early in the century the area within the city walls was still the main centre of activity. It is true that rows of terraced brick houses had replaced the orchards and fields below Union Road, along Pinhoe Road and west of the river, but shopkeepers still lived 'over the shop' and there were enough inhabited premises on the principal streets and behind Fore Street, Sidwell Street and Paris Street for the pavements to be crowded all week and for the churches to be full on Sundays. People thronged to Northernhay to listen to the band, or to Queen Street for concerts in the Civic Hall, or to London Inn Square for the Theatre Royal or the Hippodrome.

Henry Wood conducted a matinée concert at the Hippodrome in 1909. During the midday rehearsal he noticed an appalling smell. The manager explained that a visiting menagerie had made way for the orchestra, but he had not been able to move the sea-lion's tank, which was under the stage. A large supply of rotting fish was keeping the animal quiet. The audience had to put up with the stench, and the sound of splashing water during the softer passages.

110 Magistrates found it necessary to direct the police to control some nursemaids: 'The perambulator in itself is not a nuisance, but becomes so when under the care of gadding females'. Here the decorum of Northernhay is preserved.

Northernhay, Exeter.

111 In 1916 the Devonshire Regiment had one battalion of mounted infantry which trained not on horseback but on bicycles, with rifles carried as smartly as possible. The bicycles did not accompany them to France or Mesopotamia.

Fred Karno, the impresario, was born in Waterbeer Street in 1866, the son of a cabinet-maker called Westcott. Karno took over the lease of the Hippodrome, brought Marie Lloyd there, and the then unknown Charlie Chaplin. The Karno Company took Chaplin and young Stan Laurel on tour in this country, and as far as America in 1910. Their knockabout comedy led to the use of the term 'Karno' for any botched-up job. When war broke out, the drill-sergeants used it as sarcastic abuse. A marching song (coincidentally using a hymn-tune by Exeter's Samuel Sebastian Wesley) went like this:

We are Fred Karno's army,
The ragtime infantry,
We cannot shoot, we cannot fight,
What ruddy use are we?
But when we get to Berlin
The Kaiser he will say,
'Hoch, hoch, mein Gott, what a ruddy fine lot
Are the ragtime infantry'.

In December 1914 volunteers enlisted in 'Exeter's Own' regiment at the Guildhall, receiving rosettes of the city's colours. Troops passing through St David's station were given hot tea, buns and good luck cards by the mayoress and her committee. In September 1915 the king and queen visited war-wounded in the hospital. It was the first time that distinguished visitors used 'mechanical traction', and onlookers used to clattering hooves and tossing manes found that 'motor cars' glided surprisingly softly and steadily over the tarred wood blocks of the main thoroughfares. In November 1915 German guns captured at Halluch were exhibited near the castle gatehouse.

Between the wars, as car ownership spread, Exeter High Street became a notorious bottle-neck for holiday jams. The Prince of Wales opened a northern bypass along the side of the Hoopern valley in 1927, but drivers preferred to pass through the centre. The road had been

112   *Left*. This view looking down Paul Street from Queen Street shows St Paul's church (demolished 1936) on the left and the old shops and houses from many different centuries which housed a busy community until the early 1920s.

113   *Below*. In 1916 St Nicholas Priory was opened as a city museum, and Toisa's cross was erected in the garden.

114   *Right*. Lt.-Col. Sir H.C. Sclater, C.-in-C. Southern Command, presented gallantry awards at a ceremony in Northernhay Gardens on 8 May 1918, attended by mayoress Mrs. James Owen, deputy mayor Mr. Bradley Rowe, the bishops of Exeter and Crediton, Girl Guides and special guests. Some medals were collected by the widows and young sons of the fallen.

115   *Below right*. A series of 24 postcards helped to raise money for the building and endowment fund of the University College of the South West in the 1920s. This hall is now the main art gallery of the museum, but then it was the chrysalis from which the present university has burst.

116 Between St David's church and the Attwyll Palmer almshouses are the buildings of Hele's School which range from the small limestone school-house of 1850 to the redbrick extensions of 1909 and 1932 and the army huts for the overspill. The planned move to a larger site on the by-pass was to be delayed 20 years until 1959.

117 In 1907-8 it was thought that there would never be another war, and that the rows of houses off Thornton Hill could be extended across the redundant barracks. But the barracks are still there in the early 1920s. The County Cricket Ground at the top of the picture had been inaugurated in 1902 with a match against a team headed by Dr. W.G. Grace.

118 At the top of this picture from the early 1920s St James' school and church can be seen next to the Grecians' football field. Sidwell Street Methodist church is as yet unchallenged by any massive cinema auditorium. The *Acland Hotel* stands on York Road, Acland Terrace has six houses, and Summerland Street is a residential area.

119 A church dedicated to St James was built here to relieve St Sidwell's in 1836, and rebuilt in 1878-85 to a design by R. Medley Fulford. It burnt down in 1942. Its replacement stands near Stoke Hill roundabout. The foundation stone which marked its old site has been moved there too. Only the gateposts remain in St James' Road.

120 The cathedral escaped major damage during the war, possibly because enemy pilots valued it as a landmark, just as the R.A.F. would turn left for Hamburg at Cologne Cathedral. However, bombs on 24 April and 4 May 1942 destroyed the side-chapel of St James, between the S.E. choir and the chapter house.

121 Experts quickly installed steel ties across the nave to hold the main walls until the two south buttresses could be replaced; otherwise the whole cathedral could have collapsed.

122 St Mary Arches with its Norman pillars had apparently escaped the blitz of the night of 4 May, but when the sisters of St Wilfrid's took the girls in their care to a service there the next day, a smouldering fire-bomb burst into flames, destroying part of the roof. The nuns rescued the processional cross although its base was burning.

123 A similar fate befell the *Globe Hotel*, which had stood for centuries between South Street and the corner of the Cathedral Close. Weary fire-fighters and bemused office-workers saw it still standing on the morning after the blitz, but by the end of the day a raging fire had destroyed the hotel and the neighbouring shops.

124 'Bedford Circus after the Blitz' was sketched by A.C. Bown in 1942 and given to the Royal Albert Memorial Museum by the War Artists Advisory Committee. It shows the statue of the 11th Earl of Devon and the shell of Bedford Chapel in front of the cathedral, which has boarded-up windows.

125-6 The Lower Market was destroyed. It had been designed in 1835 by the local architect Charles Fowler, as was Covent Garden (cf. fig. 80). Anyone who wants to see its like must travel to Australia, where an emigrant from South Street modelled the market hall of Castlemaine, Victoria, on his childhood memories of Fowler's market.

127 Allhallows' church, Bartholomew Yard, became redundant and was used as a corset factory. One West Quarter couple were married in this church, then their daughter was employed there making parachutes, and finally their son helped to demolish it.

a condition of the sale of the Streatham Estate by the Thornton-West family to the University College, which had outgrown its premises in Gandy Street. Slum clearance projects rehoused hundreds of families in the fields round Buddle Lane and Burnthouse Lane.

The comedian Tommy Cooper lived in Fords Road, St Thomas, as a young boy in the 1930s, sometimes helping his parents sell ice-cream out of the front window of the small house. He attended Mount Radford School, a private prep school in St Leonard's.

Dame Georgiana Buller (1884-1953), only daughter of General Redvers Buller, devoted her life to hospital administration. She instigated the foundation of the orthopaedic hospital, built on former Veitch nursery ground, which was opened on 16 November 1927 by the Duke and Duchess of York and named Princess Elizabeth after their baby daughter. Rosemary Sutcliff, the brilliant author of historical novels for children, suffered from Still's Disease and spent long stretches in this hospital as a child, in a ward designed to be so healthily airy that it had no walls or ceiling. Dame Georgiana also founded the rehabilitation hospital of St Loyes in 1937, and its school of occupational therapy in 1944.

In 1931 there was a proposal to demolish six city churches as redundant now that so many residents had left the centre. St Paul's and St John's were pulled down, Allhallows was

128 In 1953 the new Bedford Street was rebuilt alongside the old one so as not to disrupt the traffic. The carriageway of Bedford Circus in the middle distance bears witness to the graceful curve of the Georgian crescents that have been cleared away.

129 The new Bedford Street is open for business, it is a rainy day in November 1953, and there is no post office yet to block the view from High Street across the city walls to Chichester Place in Southernhay.

deconsecrated, and the Nazis eventually saw to St Lawrence's and Bedford Chapel, though St Mary Major survived until the 1970s.

In the second World War Exeter did not expect to be a target, but a week after the R.A.F. had destroyed medieval Lübeck, Hitler had compiled a list of England's 'jewels' from a Baedeker guide. In the small hours of 4 May 1942 Nazi planes flew up the moonlit estuary to rain fire-bombs for 74 minutes. The blaze destroyed half of High Street and large areas around South Street, Paris Street and Sidwell Street, and such important buildings as Bampfylde House, the hall of the Vicars Choral, the 'Norman' house, Abbot's Lodge in the Close, St Luke's college and the city library.

Most of the unrivalled archives survived, behind scorched doors. Many lives were lost. The material damage from the war was finally calculated at 400 shops lost out of 1,410, and 1,500 houses out of 18,500. Willey's engineering works made some of the huge steel tanks of Mulberry Harbour for the D-day landings.

A plan for post-war reconstruction was commissioned from the town-planning expert, Thomas Sharp. His report was published as a book entitled *Exeter Phoenix* in 1946. Old etchings and photographs of surviving architectural treasures illustrated Exeter's individual character as a historic city set among green hills. Sharp believed that the 'intimacy of scale' of the pre-war streets could be recreated in modern

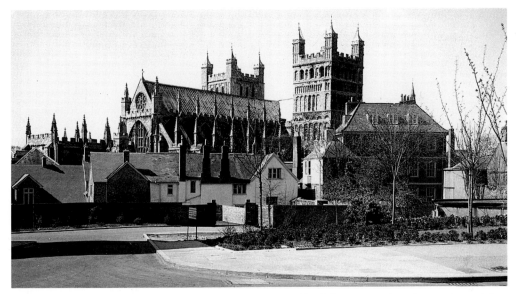

130 The view of the Cathedral Close from the new Bedford Street was thought worth retaining. The new post office was given a glazed front wall which frames this view, and the pedestrian precinct named by Princess Elizabeth was aligned to the cathedral towers. Only single-storey shops were built on this site, as Thomas Sharp had suggested.

131 The slum clearance programme continued in 1957 after a 20-year gap (apart from the unplanned clearances of 1942) and swept away many of the characteristic courts of cottages leading off Cowick Street, Sidwell Street and Magdalen Street. In Ware's Buildings, Cowick Street, each family had one all-purpose downstairs room and two bedrooms above. The WCs were grouped together in a block at a healthy distance.

132 In February 1958 the opportunity was taken to widen South Street (again), whilst carefully retaining George's Meeting and Holy Trinity on the left, and the *White Hart* and its neighbours on the right.

architecture. The ruins of St Catherine's Almshouses and the Vicars Choral Hall should remain as a memorial of war, but he did not approve of erecting replicas of destroyed buildings, or of restoring, for example, the shell of Bedford Circus. In his view, the war damage had literally cleared the way for long-needed improvements. The cathedral had been hidden from sight even from neighbouring streets. When the ruins had been bulldozed away, the cathedral stood fully revealed. Sharp suggested retaining a vista towards its north tower, from a pedestrian shopping street. The result was England's first pedestrian precinct, named Princesshay by our future queen in 1949. Sharp

also prized the glimpses of the Devon hills visible even from the centre of the city. He did not want good farming land or market gardens to be sacrificed to development. He also recommended the creation of green areas among the streets, in particular a 'green moat' of open space immediately outside the city walls, so as to expose the whole circuit to view. This has been achieved in two stretches of Southernhay at least, by opening the back gardens which abutted the wall. As for roads, Sharp saw that Exeter was at risk of 'strangulation by traffic'. He recommended an inner ring-road and a relief road for Pinhoe and Blackboy Roads (which was ready in 1949, in time for the princess to name it after her new baby, Prince Charles). Bombed-out citizens were rehoused in airy estates on green hillsides at Stoke Hill, Whipton, Exwick and Cowick. Western Way was built in the 1960s across the devastated hillside between Sidwell Street and Newtown, along a rubble viaduct dumped onto housetops in the Barnfield, and elbowing aside the 15th-century Frog Street house as it swept down to Exebridge. There was also a new outer bypass which became notorious for summer holiday tailbacks.

Indeed, the more new roads were built the more traffic came to fill them. John Betjeman spoke out against the motor-car in Exeter in the 1960s. The distinguished scholar W.G. Hoskins did the same. He had been born and educated in Exeter and loved its history and buildings. Honiton Road was to be widened, at the cost of losing two handsome historic houses 'at the entrance to Exeter', nos. 74 and 76 East Wonford Hill. In his maiden speech to the city council Hoskins said: 'I think people are more important than roads, and houses more important than cars'. Nevertheless the houses were lost. One of them had a 'highwayman's step'—one stair a different size so that a marauder would trip.

133 Old shops and houses and cramped side-cottages were cleared from Paul Street in 1921-4, leaving only the city walls and a Sunday School building. The coach station, and the bus station on the higher part, were conveniently near Queen Street railway station.

134 Cars could park under the elms of the Close until 1970. A scheme to accommodate them underground led to the demolition of the Victorian church of St Mary Major, revealing traces of the 15th-century church known from drawings, but below that—amazingly—the 11th-century apsed cathedral of Leofric, and earlier graves confirming 1600 years of continuous Christian practice on this site.

135 Until the 1970s the well-loved department store Waltons occupied a row of premises of various architectural styles at the corner of High Street and Queen Street.

136 The blitzed western end of the High Street was redeveloped with wider pavements and wider carriageways. After compulsory purchase of bomb-sites, purpose-built accommodation for chain-stores could be designed a block at a time, contrasting with the older eastern end of the street where the shops continued to adapt centuries-old merchants' dwellings on medieval burgage plots.

137 The ABC cinema was not so attractive architecturally as the Georgian *New London Inn* that it replaced, but it did provide city-centre entertainment, and the open space in front of it was a reminder of the ancient London Inn Square outside the east gate.

138 Redevelopment of the river crossing began in the 1960s with a new roundabout at the entrance to St Thomas. Shilhay, cut off by its 1,000-year-old mill leat, was still an industrial area.

139 The 1905 Exebridge remained in use during construction of the northern part of the new dual system. Exebridge North was opened in July 1969 by mayor W.J. Hallett, about 750 years after Gervase's stone bridge.

140 A view from Renslade House in August 1972 shows changes in 'Britayne' after 1,000 years. St Michael's church (1867) towers above Paradise School, being used by the art college. The cottages of Mount Dinham contrast with the high-rise Exeter College behind them. University buildings peep out of the arboretum on the skyline.

141 The University College became a full and independent university in 1955. After outgrowing the museum and adjacent buildings in Gandy Street, it scattered pink brick buildings on the hills of the former Streatham Estate. Extensive tree-planting complements the century-old arboretum that surrounds the Thornton-Wests' Italianate mansion of 1867.

142 The King's Troop, Royal Horse Artillery, pass the statue of General Redvers Buller as they ride from St David's Station to the Devon County Show at the Whipton showground in May 1968, a reminder of centuries of horse-borne soldiers, messengers and travellers who have used the streets of Exeter ever since Roman times.

The *Ben Jonson* was a familiar sight on the canal after the war. It was a small tanker which came from Southampton every month to fill the Esso storage tank by the basin. The *Ben Oliver* did the run before the war. The only other regular visitors were ships bringing timber from Sweden and salt cod from Newfoundland.

The university gained a royal charter in 1955. This gave it full independence (it had previously been an outpost of London University), including the right to award its own degrees. It expanded rapidly, now attracting scholars from many parts of the world, and a yearly invasion of young people comparable in numbers to the thousands in Vespasian's Second Augustan Legion of A.D. 50.

In 1966 the city annexed Topsham. In the reorganisation of local government Exeter was told that it would cease to be a county after 30 March 1974, and would become subject to Devon County Council and no longer have its own sheriff, but the queen did grant Exeter the right for the elected chairman of its city council to retain the title of mayor. The Exeter police force also lost its autonomy. Devon police had previously exercised authority only in certain enclaves of Exeter: the Castle, the judges' lodgings and County Hall. The amalgamation wiped out the boundaries which had served as reminders of the city's long history. But Exeter continued to play its varied rôles of capital of Devon, cathedral city, gateway to the west, always loyal. As Hooker wrote in 1587, 'the situation of this City is very pleasant and delicate, being set upon a little Hill among many Hills'. Sunlight and shadow still chase across the dumpy wooded hills, the city clusters round the cathedral towers, and the shining estuary flows out to the sea.

Further Reading

General titles
Hoskins, W.G., *Two Thousand Years in Exeter* (1960)
Thomas, P. and Warren, J., *Aspects of Exeter* (1980)

Useful titles, listed in chronological sequence
Todd, M., *The South-West to A.D. 1000* (1987)
Henderson, C., 'The Roman walls of Exeter', *Devon Archaeology*, vol. 2 (1984)
Connor, P.W., *Anglo-Saxon Exeter* (1993)
Swanton, M. (ed.), *Exeter Cathedral—a Celebration* (1991)
Henderson, C., 'The archaeology of Exeter quay', *Devon Archaeology*, vol. 4 (1991)
Youings, J., *Tuckers' Hall* (1968)
Stoyle, M., 'Exeter in the Civil War', *Devon Archaeology*, vol. 6 (1995)
Newton, R., *Eighteenth-century Exeter* (1984)
Newton, R., *Victorian Exeter* (1968)
Clapp, B.W., *The University of Exeter: a History* (1982)

Specialist titles
Meller, H., *Exeter Architecture* (1989)
Minchington, W., *Life to the City* (1987)
Ryton, J., *Banks and Banknotes of Exeter 1769-1906* (1984)
Levine, G. and Eustace, D., *Secrets of a Garden City* (1990)
Exeter Civic Society, *Discovering Exeter* series: *St David's* (1981); *St Leonard's* (1982); *Heavitree* (1983); *Pennsylvania* (1984); *Sidwell Street* (1986); *West of the River* (1989); *Lost Churches* (1995)

Index

Figures in bold refer to illustration page numbers.